YASIR ARAFAT

MENACHEM BEGIN

TONY BLAIR

GEORGE W. BUSH

JIMMY CARTER

VICENTE FOX

SADDAM HUSSEIN

HOSNI MUBARAK

VLADIMIR PUTIN

MOHAMMED REZA PAHLAVI

ANWAR SADAT

THE SAUDI ROYAL FAMILY

Hosni Mubarak

Vicki Cox

CHELSEA HOUSE
PUBLISHERS
A Haights Cross Communications Company

Philadelphia

Frontispiece: Hosni Mubarak brought economic and social stability to Egypt when he became president after Anwar Sadat's assassination in 1981.

CHELSEA HOUSE PUBLISHERS

EDITOR IN CHIEF Sally Cheney
DIRECTOR OF PRODUCTION Kim Shinners
CREATIVE MANAGER Takeshi Takahashi
MANUFACTURING MANAGER Diann Grasse

Staff for HOSNI MUBARAK

EDITOR Lee Marcott
ASSOCIATE EDITOR Bill Conn
PRODUCTION ASSISTANT Jaimie Winkler
PICTURE RESEARCH 21st Century Publishing and Communications, Inc.
SERIES AND COVER DESIGNER Takeshi Takahashi
LAYOUT 21st Century Publishing and Communications, Inc.

A Haights Cross Communications ⟋ Company

http://www.chelseahouse.com

First Printing

1 3 5 7 9 8 6 4 2

Library of Congress Cataloging-in-Publication Data

Cox, Vicki.
  Hosni Mubarak / Vicki Cox.
    p. cm.—(Major world leaders)
Summary: A biography of Egyptian President Hosni Mubarak, a military hero who became president after the assassination of Anwar Sadat, set against the history of Egypt and its lengthy and bloody battle with Israel.
Includes bibliographical references and index.
  ISBN 0-7910-6942-7
  1. Mubåarak, Muòhammad òHusnåi, 1928– —Juvenile literature. 2. Presidents—Egypt—Biography—Juvenile literature. [1. Mubåarak, Muòhammad òHusnåi, 1928–2. Presidents—Egypt.] I. Title. II. Series.
DT107.87 .C69 2002
962.05'092—dc21
                                        2002007153

TABLE OF CONTENTS

On Leadership

Arthur M. Schlesinger, jr.

Leadership, it may be said, is really what makes the world go round. Love no doubt smoothes the passage; but love is a private transaction between consenting adults. Leadership is a public transaction with history. The idea of leadership affirms the capacity of individuals to move, inspire, and mobilize masses of people so that they act together in pursuit of an end. Sometimes leadership serves good purposes, sometimes bad; but whether the end is benign or evil, great leaders are those men and women who leave their personal stamp on history.

Now, the very concept of leadership implies the proposition that individuals can make a difference. This proposition has never been universally accepted. From classical times to the present day, eminent thinkers have regarded individuals as no more than the agents and pawns of larger forces, whether the gods and goddesses of the ancient world or, in the modern era, race, class, nation, the dialectic, the will of the people, the spirit of the times, history itself. Against such forces, the individual dwindles into insignificance.

So contends the thesis of historical determinism. Tolstoy's great novel *War and Peace* offers a famous statement of the case. Why, Tolstoy asked, did millions of men in the Napoleonic Wars, denying their human feelings and their common sense, move back and forth across Europe slaughtering their fellows? "The war," Tolstoy answered, "was bound to happen simply because it was bound to happen." All prior history determined it. As for leaders, they, Tolstoy said, "are but the labels that serve to give a name to an end and, like labels, they have the least possible connection with the event." The greater the leader, "the more conspicuous the inevitability and the predestination of every act he commits." The leader, said Tolstoy, is "the slave of history."

Determinism takes many forms. Marxism is the determinism of class. Nazism the determinism of race. But the idea of men and women as the slaves of history runs athwart the deepest human instincts. Rigid determinism abolishes the idea of human freedom—the assumption of free choice that underlies every move we make, every word we speak, every thought we think. It abolishes the idea of human responsibility,

since it is manifestly unfair to reward or punish people for actions that are by definition beyond their control. No one can live consistently by any deterministic creed. The Marxist states prove this themselves by their extreme susceptibility to the cult of leadership.

More than that, history refutes the idea that individuals make no difference. In December 1931 a British politician crossing Fifth Avenue in New York City between 76th and 77th Streets around 10:30 P.M. looked in the wrong direction and was knocked down by an automobile—a moment, he later recalled, of a man aghast, a world aglare: "I do not understand why I was not broken like an eggshell or squashed like a gooseberry." Fourteen months later an American politician, sitting in an open car in Miami, Florida, was fired on by an assassin; the man beside him was hit. Those who believe that individuals make no difference to history might well ponder whether the next two decades would have been the same had Mario Constasino's car killed Winston Churchill in 1931 and Giuseppe Zangara's bullet killed Franklin Roosevelt in 1933. Suppose, in addition, that Lenin had died of typhus in Siberia in 1895 and that Hitler had been killed on the western front in 1916. What would the 20th century have looked like now?

For better or for worse, individuals do make a difference. "The notion that a people can run itself and its affairs anonymously," wrote the philosopher William James, "is now well known to be the silliest of absurdities. Mankind does nothing save through initiatives on the part of inventors, great or small, and imitation by the rest of us—these are the sole factors in human progress. Individuals of genius show the way, and set the patterns, which common people then adopt and follow."

Leadership, James suggests, means leadership in thought as well as in action. In the long run, leaders in thought may well make the greater difference to the world. "The ideas of economists and political philosophers, both when they are right and when they are wrong," wrote John Maynard Keynes, "are more powerful than is commonly understood. Indeed the world is ruled by little else. Practical men, who believe themselves to be quite exempt from any intellectual influences, are usually the slaves of some defunct economist. . . . The power of vested interests is vastly exaggerated compared with the gradual encroachment of ideas."

But, as Woodrow Wilson once said, "Those only are leaders of men, in the general eye, who lead in action. . . . It is at their hands that new thought gets its translation into the crude language of deeds." Leaders in thought often invent in solitude and obscurity, leaving to later generations the tasks of imitation. Leaders in action—the leaders portrayed in this series—have to be effective in their own time.

And they cannot be effective by themselves. They must act in response to the rhythms of their age. Their genius must be adapted, in a phrase from William James, "to the receptivities of the moment." Leaders are useless without followers. "There goes the mob," said the French politician, hearing a clamor in the streets. "I am their leader. I must follow them." Great leaders turn the inchoate emotions of the mob to purposes of their own. They seize on the opportunities of their time, the hopes, fears, frustrations, crises, potentialities. They succeed when events have prepared the way for them, when the community is awaiting to be aroused, when they can provide the clarifying and organizing ideas. Leadership completes the circuit between the individual and the mass and thereby alters history.

It may alter history for better or for worse. Leaders have been responsible for the most extravagant follies and most monstrous crimes that have beset suffering humanity. They have also been vital in such gains as humanity has made in individual freedom, religious and racial tolerance, social justice, and respect for human rights.

There is no sure way to tell in advance who is going to lead for good and who for evil. But a glance at the gallery of men and women in MAJOR WORLD LEADERS suggests some useful tests.

One test is this: Do leaders lead by force or by persuasion? By command or by consent? Through most of history leadership was exercised by the divine right of authority. The duty of followers was to defer and to obey. "Theirs not to reason why/Theirs but to do and die." On occasion, as with the so-called enlightened despots of the 18th century in Europe, absolutist leadership was animated by humane purposes. More often, absolutism nourished the passion for domination, land, gold, and conquest and resulted in tyranny.

The great revolution of modern times has been the revolution of equality. "Perhaps no form of government," wrote the British historian James Bryce in his study of the United States, *The American Commonwealth*, "needs great leaders so much as democracy." The idea that all people should be equal in their legal condition has undermined the old structure of authority, hierarchy, and deference. The revolution of equality has had two contrary effects on the nature of leadership. For equality, as Alexis de Tocqueville pointed out in his great study *Democracy in America*, might mean equality in servitude as well as equality in freedom.

"I know of only two methods of establishing equality in the political world," Tocqueville wrote. "Rights must be given to every citizen, or none at all to anyone . . . save one, who is the master of all." There was no middle ground "between the sovereignty of all and the absolute power of one man." In his astonishing prediction of 20th-century totalitarian dictatorship, Tocqueville explained how the revolution of equality could lead to the *Führerprinzip* and more terrible absolutism than the world had ever known.

But when rights are given to every citizen and the sovereignty of all is established, the problem of leadership takes a new form, becomes more exacting than ever before. It is easy to issue commands and enforce them by the rope and the stake, the concentration camp and the *gulag*. It is much harder to use argument and achievement to overcome opposition and win consent. The Founding Fathers of the United States understood the difficulty. They believed that history had given them the opportunity to decide, as Alexander Hamilton wrote in the first Federalist Paper, whether men are indeed capable of basing government on "reflection and choice, or whether they are forever destined to depend . . . on accident and force."

Government by reflection and choice called for a new style of leadership and a new quality of followership. It required leaders to be responsive to popular concerns, and it required followers to be active and informed participants in the process. Democracy does not eliminate emotion from politics; sometimes it fosters demagoguery; but it is confident that, as the greatest of democratic leaders put it, you cannot fool all of the people all of the time. It measures leadership by results and retires those who overreach or falter or fail.

It is true that in the long run despots are measured by results too. But they can postpone the day of judgment, sometimes indefinitely, and in the meantime they can do infinite harm. It is also true that democracy is no guarantee of virtue and intelligence in government, for the voice of the people is not necessarily the voice of God. But democracy, by assuring the right of opposition, offers built-in resistance to the evils inherent in absolutism. As the theologian Reinhold Niebuhr summed it up, "Man's capacity for justice makes democracy possible, but man's inclination to justice makes democracy necessary."

A second test for leadership is the end for which power is sought. When leaders have as their goal the supremacy of a master race or the promotion of totalitarian revolution or the acquisition and exploitation of colonies or the protection of greed and privilege or the preservation of personal power, it is likely that their leadership will do little to advance the cause of humanity. When their goal is the abolition of slavery, the liberation of women, the enlargement of opportunity for the poor and powerless, the extension of equal rights to racial minorities, the defense of the freedoms of expression and opposition, it is likely that their leadership will increase the sum of human liberty and welfare.

Leaders have done great harm to the world. They have also conferred great benefits. You will find both sorts in this series. Even "good" leaders must be regarded with a certain wariness. Leaders are not demigods; they put on their trousers one leg after another just like ordinary mortals. No leader is infallible, and every leader needs to be reminded of this at regular intervals. Irreverence irritates leaders but is their salvation. Unquestioning submission corrupts leaders and demeans followers. Making a cult of a leader is always a mistake. Fortunately hero worship generates its own antidote. "Every hero," said Emerson, "becomes a bore at last."

The signal benefit the great leaders confer is to embolden the rest of us to live according to our own best selves, to be active, insistent, and resolute in affirming our own sense of things. For great leaders attest to the reality of human freedom against the supposed inevitabilities of history. And they attest to the wisdom and power that may lie within the most unlikely of us, which is why Abraham Lincoln remains the supreme example of great leadership. A great leader, said Emerson, exhibits new possibilities to all humanity. "We feed on genius . . . . Great men exist that there may be greater men."

Great leaders, in short, justify themselves by emancipating and empowering their followers. So humanity struggles to master its destiny, remembering with Alexis de Tocqueville: "It is true that around every man a fatal circle is traced beyond which he cannot pass; but within the wide verge of that circle he is powerful and free; as it is with man, so with communities." ■

Egyptian Vice President Hosni Mubarak (second from right) rides in a military parade in Cairo, Egypt, in honor of the 1973 Yom Kippur War. With him is President Anwar Sadat (saluting), who was later shot while viewing this parade on October 6, 1981.

Out of the Shadows

His military uniform covered with ribbons, Hosni Mubarak sat down beside his president, Anwar Sadat, to enjoy the parade. On this day, October 6, 1981, he was supposed to celebrate Egypt's victory over Israel in the 1973 Yom Kippur War. Just as on the seven previous Octobers, Vice President Mubarak deserved every salute that the military who passed by the reviewing stand could give him. He was a hero of the 1973 conflict. Without his brilliant surprise attack on the Israelis, Egypt could never have crossed the Suez Canal and engaged the Israelis on the Sinai Peninsula. Without the 1973 war, Egypt could not have regained the pride it had lost after Israel won the 1948 and 1967 wars. Without the victory over the Israelis, Sadat could never have negotiated with them or with the rest of the world from a position of authority.

THE CELEBRATION

When Vice President Mubarak left home early that October morning, he expected to enjoy the annual reliving of this glorious moment with Egypt's president. There was to be a 90-minute military show of the troops, their military equipment, and their might. The president and vice president expected a technicolor air show. They wanted the people to see how many foreign countries had sold them sophisticated weapons.

Mubarak and Sadat settled into the concrete-and-glass reviewing stand. Behind them sat other government officials, 1,000 invited ambassadors, and journalists from other countries. Mrs. Mubarak and Mrs. Sadat were also watching. Sadat saluted the turbaned Hagganah Camel troops that patrol parts of the Egyptian frontier. He puffed on his pipe. Under the midday sun, Sadat removed his hat to wipe off the sweat, placing it on the rail in front of him. Mubarak and Sadat laughed and talked easily with one another.

Fireworks exploded overhead. Mortars fired parachutes carrying small Egyptian flags and portraits of Sadat. Jet fighters flew by; their shrieking engines made spectators cover their ears. Skydivers floated to the ground, spiraling in circles until the sky itself was a grandiose stage to honor Egypt's reclaimed respect in the world.

During the time of the pharaohs, Egypt had been a center of trade, culture, art, and learning. But in recent years, it had been humiliated time and again by its arch enemy, Israel. After Israel declared independence in 1948, Egypt and four other Arab countries had declared war on the new country, only to be defeated. In the 1967 war, the Israelis had not only crushed Egypt's military in six days, they had captured new territory, including Egypt's Sinai Peninsula. Then, six years later, thanks to the cunning of Vice President Mubarak's air attacks, Egyptian troops had stormed across the Suez Canal and the 47-foot earthen barrier that Israel had claimed was impenetrable. Egypt humbled the mighty Israeli army and regained its ancient pride.

ASSASSINS' ATTACK

No one expected trouble on this special October day. Under the clear sky and warm sun, Mubarak and the president were among friends—the loyal troops Sadat called "his children." Recalled Mubarak, " . . . we sat in our places there, we started to see the show, and we discussed what we were going to do on the 25th of April [when Israel is due to return the remainder of the Sinai]. . . . President Sadat was always thinking what kind of ceremony he wanted. . . . While the show was passing, it was giving him new ideas."

Mubarak and Sadat talked about the approaching historical event—when Israel would make good its promise to return to Egypt the last section of the Sinai Peninsula. Both men were looking up, as French-made Mirage 5-E jets flew overhead, ribboning the sky with red, orange, blue, and green smoke. They paid no attention to a particular truck near the end of the parade—just 1 among 72 Soviet-made flatbeds passing by the reviewing stand with their North Korean armor-piercing artillery. But this truck pulled away from its position in the next-to-the-last row and stopped. Those who might have noticed could easily have dismissed it as another mechanical breakdown. There had been several already.

"He said, 'I have decided to promote some officers who participated in the '73 war,'" said Mubarak, remembering the last words his president spoke. Khaled Islambouli, a young junior lieutenant stepped from the truck cab and approached the stands.

"I saw the President standing up," recalls Mubarak. "Whenever he stands, we have to stand and in a second I just saw the image of someone throwing something."

Instead of giving a snappy salute, the young man threw a grenade at Sadat. It exploded, throwing glass and shrapnel into the reviewing stand.

"I was pushed away, and I tried to push the President down," said Mubarak. "Other people tried, but he resisted. He couldn't believe such an event could happen. For us, this is the first time in our history. . . . We're not used to such things."

More grenades were thrown. Three landed in the reviewing stand but did not detonate. The presidential security guards and members of the army seemed helpless as three accomplices jumped from a truck, firing submachine guns and flinging concussion and fragmentation grenades. Sadat turned to his bodyguards and pointed.

The assassins ran to the reviewing stand, firing their guns. One reportedly yelled, "Glory for Egypt! Attack!" Islambouli yelled, "Pharaoh! Pharaoh!" Others say he yelled at Mubarak and the minister of defense, "Get out of my way. I only want this son of a dog."

Nothing and no one prevented the assassins' approach. The guerrilla guards who usually stood near the president were not there. The sharpshooters usually positioned on the roof were absent also. Stunned by what they were watching, some soldiers froze in their places. Others ducked and ran for cover. The crowd ran for the rear exits.

Two terrorists ran to the front of the stand, pumping bullets straight at the presidential party. Another fired from the side. Bullets shattered the reviewing stand glass in front of Sadat. Bullets thudded into concrete walls. Defense Minister Abu Ghazala, seated to the president's left was hit in the face and arm.

"I felt the bullets flying all around me. I could feel the heat of them," he said. "Twice I thought it was all over: when I saw the grenade flying toward me, and when I saw a gun barrel

Dressed in an Egyptian army uniform, an assassin fires a rifle into the reviewing stand during an Egyptian military parade honoring the Yom Kippur War of 1973. The attack killed President Sadat and six others, and wounded many—including Hosni Mubarak.

right in my face, just five feet away from me."

Vice President Mubarak who had been at the president's right, was hit in the hand.

Sadat's bodyguard finally fired back, shouting to Sadat, "Get your head down! Get your head down!"

Sadat, hit in the neck, thigh, forearm, and twice in the chest, gasped and fell. His personal secretary, who had been seated behind Sadat, threw himself between Sadat and the gunfire. He tried to cover Sadat with wooden chairs. He, too, was wounded. Seconds later, Anwar Sadat lay on his back, his face covered with blood, his fate obvious. "I saw then that he was finished," said Mubarak.

The barrage of bullets lasted 45 seconds. When it was over, chairs were overturned, and people were lying on the ground. Scores were wounded. Seven people were dead. Spectators stood over the carnage, staring in shocked disbelief. Soldiers, themselves in tears, restrained the crowd.

WHO WAS RESPONSIBLE?

The assassins could have acted for one of several different groups. For, despite his acclaim as a visionary world leader, Anwar Sadat had many enemies, both inside and outside Egypt.

Even his own people, struggling to buy food and find a place to live, could have been responsible for the bullets. Unemployment was high. Overcrowding was higher. Inflation hovered near 30 percent. Although Egypt's import bill for food was $8 million a day, it was not enough. Sadat had opened Egypt to Western investors, but only a very few Egyptians profited from them.

The bullets could have belonged to assassins from another Arab country. Sadat was hated by his Arab neighbors for initiating peace talks with Israel in 1978. The Arabs had never admitted that Israel had a right to exist as a country. After Sadat and Israeli Prime Minister Menachem Begin forged a

The reviewing stand after the barrage of machine gun bullets and grenades that killed Egyptian President Anwar Sadat and others.

peace treaty, the Arabs had expelled Egypt from the Arab League, placing economic and political sanctions on Egypt. When news of Sadat's murder reached them, Lebanese militants celebrated in the streets, firing assault rifles in the air. A security chief for the Palestine Liberation Organization (PLO) said he would "shake the hand of him who pulled the trigger." The Syrian government, once Sadat's ally, called him a "traitor." Palestinians passed out candy to children. Lybia's Colonel Muammar Qaddafi boasted, "From now on, no one will take the same course followed by Anwar Sadat."

When the gunfire began, Mrs. Mubarak and Mrs. Sadat had been pulled to the floor of the glassed-in reviewing box. Amid the screams and children crying, Mrs. Sadat turned to Mrs. Mubarak. "It is the Muslim fanatics," she said, as bullets continued their tattoo through the air. She was right.

Religious fundamentalists felt that Sadat had betrayed the Koran (the holy book of their religion) by his Western way, because he negotiated with Israel. They resented the sanctuary he offered to the dying shah, who had been deposed by militants in Iran. Most Egyptians believe their religion should be an important part of their lives, but the radical Islamic groups wanted the Koran to structure even the country's government and society. They hated Sadat's policy, "No religion in politics and no politics in religion."

In August of 1981, Vice President Mubarak and Interior Minister Nabawi Ismail had warned Sadat that assassination attempts were highly possible. After rioting began between the Christian Copts and the Muslim fundamentalists in September, Sadat arrested 1,500 dissidents—political opponents—and religious extremists. He appointed himself prime minister and president for life. Egyptian politics were far from peaceful.

MUBARAK, THE NEW LEADER

The charismatic and flamboyant Sadat strode through the swirl of hatred as if it hardly existed. At his side, the quiet and loyal Vice President Mubarak had hardly been noticed—

until October 6. In less than a minute, whether he wanted it or not, Hosni Mubarak acquired a new destiny. He was Egypt's next leader.

Mubarak was whisked away to the Maadi Military Hospital nine miles away, where his wounded hand was tended and bandaged. Sadat was carried to a Gazelle helicopter and also rushed to the hospital. Mrs. Sadat arrived at the hospital shortly after.

"The doctors are doing their best in the operating room," Mubarak told her. Government ministers, friends, and Sadat's family awaited word about Sadat's condition. The doctors worked an hour and a half to save their leader, administering massive blood transfusions and open-chest massage. But it was hopeless from the beginning. Sadat had arrived at the hospital with no pulse; his eyes were open and fixed. Dead on arrival.

Finally, Mrs. Sadat went to her husband. His uniform sleeve has been ripped for the blood transfusions. His eyes had been closed and his jaw bound shut. She sent for her daughters and their husbands, but requested that no one else see Sadat's body.

Returning to the waiting room Mrs. Sadat told Mubarak, "Mr. President, Anwar Sadat is gone. He is not living anymore. This is God's will. But Egypt is still living and is in mortal danger. Now it is you who must lead us."

Mubarak, still in shock, did not move, even when ministers filed out of the room to hold an emergency meeting. A minister returned to urge him to go with them. Finally, as if coming out of a trance, Mubarak stood and left.

The 30 ministers agreed to follow the rules of succession. The Speaker of Parliament issued a one-year state of emergency and named Mubarak acting president until formalities could be arranged to elect a new president.

Egyptian television had been suspended when the shooting began. After 15 minutes, a bulletin announced that Sadat,

Mubarak, and Defense Minister Abu Ghazala had left the parade. Later, another bulletin revealed that Sadat and some aides had been injured. In the silence, rumors flew. Some thought a full-fledged revolution was underway. Another scenario placed the assassins at Assiut University, where they were killing anyone who opposed them.

Seven hours later, Vice President Hosni Mubarak appeared on Egyptian television.

"Our leader, loved by millions, the hero of war and peace, is dead," he said. "God has ordered that Sadat should die on a day which itself is a symbol of him, among his soldiers, heroes, and people, proudly celebrating the day on which the Arab world regained its dignity."

The next night the Parliament nominated Hosni Mubarak as president, prime minister, and commander in chief of the armed forces and voted that he remain vice president.

No one really believed the assassination could be the work of a few. Even in her grief, Mrs. Sadat wondered if the assassins' frontal attack might have been a ruse for someone in the reviewing stand to shoot the president from behind. To inspect the bullets that killed Sadat, she insisted she and Gamal, their son, attend the autopsy. No one would permit it until Gamal called Mubarak, who sympathetically agreed to her request. "I cannot prevent her," Mubarak told Gamal. "He was her husband. I can't tell her no."

Anwar Sadat was buried in the Tomb of the Unknown Soldier, directly across from the reviewing stand where he lost his life. Kings, princes, premiers, and three American presidents attended. Representatives from Europe, the Soviet Union, and Africa came to pay their respects. Among the Arab leaders, only Sudan, Oman, and Somalia sent representatives. The others refused to be near Prime Minister Menachem Begin of Israel. Acting President Hosni Mubarak, holding the hand of Sadat's son, led the funeral procession.

No one knew much about 53-year-old Hosni Mubarak, who would lead the Arab Republic of Egypt. The United States and Israel were uneasy. The Arab world was curious. Egyptians were nervous. All the world waited, wondering what Hosni Mubarak would do.

This map of the Middle East shows the United Arab Republic of Egypt, Hosni Mubarak's homeland, and it's neighboring countries. Egypt is located in northeast Africa.

Of History and History Books

Muhammed Hosni Mubarak's homeland is a country of palm trees, pharaohs, great civilizations, and violent conflicts. The United Arab Republic of Egypt is located in Africa, where Africa and Asia meet. The Mediterranean Sea is to its north; the Red Sea and the Suez Canal lie east. Sudan and Libya border its south and west. Israel is northeast, bordering the Sinai Peninsula.

About the combined size of California and Texas, Egypt's 386,000 square miles are split into two geographic regions. Ninety-six percent of the country is barren desert, sparsely populated by wandering nomads. Part of the Sahara, the Western (or Libyan) Desert covers about two-thirds of Egypt. The Eastern (or Arabian) Desert extends the Sahara east of the Nile River. The Nubian Desert spreads from Sudan into Egypt's southeast. The Sinai Peninsula is separated from the rest of Egypt by the Suez Canal. The Qattara Depression in northwestern

Egypt is Africa's lowest point at 436 feet below sea level. Egypt's highest mountain, Mount Jabal Katrinah, rises 8,000 feet and is the biblical Mount Sinai, where Moses received the Ten Commandments. The regions temperatures range from 30° to 120° F.

The smaller region, making up about 4 percent of Egypt, centers around the world's longest river—the Nile. The Nile River begins at the Luvironza River, more than 3,000 miles from Egypt's border. The White Nile runs north out of the mountains and is joined by the tumultuous Blue Nile at Khartoum. The Nile empties into the Mediterranean Sea, after having flowed through Egypt for more than 900 miles and drained 1.1 million square miles (or about one-tenth of the entire African continent). Its journey nourishes the Nile Valley, a narrow strip of land 5 to 20 miles wide south of Cairo and 15 miles wide at Cairo. At Cairo, the Nile fans out into the Nile Delta, a triangular-shaped area about 100 miles in length and 155 miles wide. Ninety-eight percent of Egypt's 68 million people live in this area. Using both ancient methods and modern technologies, farmers grow wheat, cotton, rice, and vegetables. Long ago, Greek historian Herodotus said that Egypt was "the gift of the river," since it is Egypt's only source of both water and nourishment.

Before Menes united Egypt in 3100 B.C., Egypt had been two separate regions. The ruler of Upper Egypt (the southern portion of modern Egypt) wore a white crown, which represented the dazzling white land of the southern region. The ruler of Lower Egypt (the northern section near the Mediterranean Sea) wore a red crown, which represented the color of Nile mud. When Menes slipped on a new double crown of red and white, Egypt's First Dynasty and the period of the Old Kingdom began.

THE RULE OF THE PHARAOHS

During the 30 dynasties of the god-king pharaohs, Egyptians ruled Egypt. They invented paper from papyrus

One of the greatest achievements of the Egyptian dynasties is the Great Pyramid at Giza—the largest stone building in the world.

reeds, created record keeping, developed irrigation techniques, mummified the dead, devised a numeric system, and built the Great Pyramid. Khufu's tomb at Giza, built 479 feet high with nearly 2½ million limestone blocks, is the largest stone building in the world.

During the First Intermediate Period, warring families fought each other for the throne until princes from Thebes reunited Egypt in 2,050 B.C. and fought Nubia and Palestine. By 1,800 B.C., the Hyksos invaded from western Asia and conquered the Egyptians with their new war technology— horse-drawn chariots. Queen Hatshepsut increased trade. Her successor, Thutmose II, reconquered Palestine and Syria and expanded Egypt to the Euphrates River.

The religious conflicts that disturb Egypt today are nothing new. During the Early New Kingdom, Amenhotep IV tried to decree the worship of just one God, Aton. Occupied with domestic affairs, the king lost Syria to the Hittites. Once again the priests of the old religion rebelled, forcing the new pharaoh, Tutankhamen, to go back to worshipping many gods.

SHIFTING RULE

After the last of the pharaohs fell to invasion in 525 B.C., Egypt shifted, like the desert, from one empire to another. The Persians under Cyrus the Great ruled Egypt for 200 years. In 333 B.C., Alexander the Great ousted the Persians. The Greeks established Alexandria as the Mediterranean world's intellectual center. Alexander accepted Egyptian gods and sought military advice from Egypt's soothsayers. A long line of kings named Ptolemy followed Alexander. For 300 years, their quarreling and corruption inspired many Egyptian revolts. During the time of Queen Cleopatra, the Greeks asked the Romans to quell Egyptian uprisings. Egyptians were a conquered people, but they struggled against their fate.

Queen Cleopatra died in 30 B.C., and Egypt was ruled by the Romans until A.D. 642 when Patriarch Gregory surrendered to Muslim Arabs. During this Byzantine period, Christianity grew. Egyptians, who once worshipped several hundred gods, easily accepted one more. Alexandria became a center of the Christian faith in Egypt. And the Coptic Church, the Egyptian branch of Christianity, became important. Although Theodosius I closed the old temples and made Christianity the official faith of the empire, he never succeeded in completely eliminating worship of the ancient gods.

The Muslims then overran Egypt in A.D. 639. The Arab language replaced Greek and Coptic. For three centuries, Egypt was ruled first by Arab governors and then by the Turks of the Ottoman Empire.

In A.D. 969, Shiite Muslims (Fatimids) swept in from

North Africa. They established a new capital called El-Qahira (Cairo). Under the Fatimids' rule, Egypt expanded to southern Syria, North Africa, and part of the Arabian Peninsula. Art, architecture, and culture flourished.

Two hundred years later, the Fatimid governors were overthrown by Saladin. He ruled Egypt for only two decades, fighting the crusaders and squashing several civil wars.

For the next three centuries, the Mamelukes (or Mamluks) ruled Egypt. They constantly bickered and plotted against whomever sat on the throne. They were harsh rulers who treated Egyptian *fellahin* (peasants) terribly. Although the Ottoman Turks invaded and occupied Egypt for 300 years, they were only interested in collecting taxes from Egypt and allowed the Mamelukes to continue governing. The Egyptians resisted both the Turkish language and culture.

THE ARRIVAL OF THE FRENCH AND THE TURKS

In 1798, Napoleon Bonaparte liberated a reluctant Egypt. Landing with 40,000 men, he sought to thwart Britain by interfering with its trade routes and communications with the East. He defeated the Mamelukes, but the English found his fleet and destroyed it. With the sultan of Turkey and the British pursuing him, Napoleon left Egypt. The scholars and scientists he brought with him during his brief three years renewed the world's interest in Egyptian culture.

In 1799, a French engineering officer discovered the Rosetta Stone. The inscriptions on the 4-by-2-foot black rock enabled scholars to translate hieroglyphics. Unlocking the Egyptian writing left on temple walls and scrolls of papyrus was a historical liberation more significant than any military campaign would ever be.

With Napoleon's withdrawal, the Ottomans returned to power. In 1805, the sultan appointed Muhammad Ali as *pasha* (ruler) of Egypt. This founder of modern Egypt brought new strains of cotton from India and introduced sugar cane. He dug new irrigation ditches and put specialists to work developing other crops. He encouraged Egyptians to study abroad and invited Western experts to lecture in Egypt. Muhammad Ali warred against the Ottomans, but their allies, British and French, fought against him. In 1841, the Ottomans appointed Ali permanent viceroy of Egypt, a designation that passed to his heirs.

THE SUEZ CANAL AND BRITAIN

One of Muhammad Ali's relatives, Isma'il Pasha, governed during the construction of the Suez Canal in 1862. This passageway between the Red Sea and the Mediterranean Sea was vital to the world's economy. More than anything else, it ensured that others would control Egypt's destiny.

For its part in constructing the canal, France received a 99-year concession to run it. When the Suez Canal was completed on November 17, 1869, the French luxury liner, *Aigle*, was the first to enter the waterway, carrying Empress Eugenie, wife of Napoleon III. The Suez Canal provided a quicker route to Britain's prize colony, India. Realizing the canal was an economic disaster for Egypt, Britain offered to buy Egypt's 44 percent of the canal. Isma'il sold Egypt's portion of the canal, a shortsighted decision that gave away Egypt's most precious asset. The vast amount of money generated by the Suez Canal was detoured into British and French treasuries instead of Egypt's.

Egypt's weakened economy and a revolt of army officers against British rule in 1879 were just the excuses Britain needed to intervene and begin yet another foreign occupation of Egypt. Egypt became known as the "Veiled Protectorate" because Britain exercised so much control over its government. During World War I, Great Britain protected the Suez Canal with its troops and used Egypt as a base for its military operations. By the end of World War I, Egypt wanted its independence. A political group called *Wafd*, meaning "delegation," organized

The Suez Canal connects the Red Sea to the Mediterranean Sea, and offered a shorter passage to India from England. The opening ceremony of the canal in 1869 marked the beginning of British involvement in Egypt's domestic affairs, which lasted until Egypt gained independence in 1922.

opposition to the British, presenting the differences made between the Europeans and Egyptians. Foreigners didn't have to obey Egyptian laws. Legal matters were settled in a special court for foreigners. Remembering the proud pharaohs, Egyptians were humiliated by such lack of respect. Egyptians had had enough. After over 3,700 years under the thumb of some other country's government, Egyptians wanted to chart their own destiny. The *Wafd* pressed the British to loosen its control over Egypt and in 1918 organized a revolt.

Finally in 1922, the same year in which Howard Carter discovered King Tutankhamen's tomb, Great Britain relented. It allowed the formation of the Kingdom of Egypt and permitted King Fuad to ascend the throne, retaining the right to keep troops in Egypt and to protect the Suez Canal. In 1936, King Fuad died, and his son Farouk replaced him. In the Anglo-Egyptian treaty, Britain agreed to Egypt's independence, provided that Britain could continue until 1956 to protect the Suez Canal.

YOUNG HOSNI MUBARAK

Egypt had been operating under its own constitution and parliament for only six years when Hosni Mubarak was born on May 4, 1928. Egypt's political turmoil had little effect on young Hosni. Living about 80 miles north of Cairo in the Nile Delta province of Menoufiya, Hosni didn't see his king growing fat on his own indulgences. He was more concerned about whether he would get an egg for breakfast and rice and boiled lamb for dinner.

Supported by the English, King Farouk inspired little loyalty from his own people. He lived in opulence, acquiring yachts, airplanes, and over 200 cars. In addition to his personal self-indulgence, Farouk did not govern Egypt well. He could not control inflation. He assigned unfair taxes. Prices rose twice as fast as wages. Government workers, who made up the middle class, earned only about $15 per month. The very few rich owned great parcels of land. The millions of poor, the *fellahin*, tended these estates, earning about $4 a month. The *fellahin* would say, "We are like the needle. We clothe others, but we ourselves stay naked."

Hosni was lucky. His father was not a *fellah*. A strict disciplinarian, Mubarak's father was an inspector in the Ministry of Justice. Hosni, his parents, three brothers, and sister lived in Kafr-El Meselha. Although 70 percent of Egypt was illiterate, in Mubarak's province of Menoufiya almost everyone could read and write. That was because in 1918, Abeel-Aziz Fahmi Pasha made the province a test case for his theory that education was the real answer to Egypt's troubles. Its citizens were educated, and consequently many government officials came from the province.

Mubarak was a quiet loner, and school was serious business to him. He was a good—not brilliant—student. Sometimes he helped his friends study after school. He loved hockey. Only a few stories about his childhood are known. One story concerns how he marched through his town on the way to a hockey match and used his hockey stick to fend off wild dogs.

After six years in the primary grades, Hosni attended three years at the lower secondary level and three years at the upper secondary stage. Going on to a university level education depended on having good scores on his final exams.

Hosni was in the middle of his studies when World War II began. In 1942, Germany and Italy invaded Egypt. To no one's surprise, they were after the Suez Canal. The Egyptians welcomed them, thinking they might provide a way of retaliating against the British, but the Allies defeated Rommel ("Desert Fox, "commander of German forces in North Africa in World War II) at the Battle of El Alamein, just 65 miles from Alexandria.

The year when Mubarak entered Egyptian Military Academy in Cairo, the Arab world blew apart. In 1947, the United Nations, of which Egypt had been a founding member, voted to divide Palestine into Jewish and Arab states. Arabs everywhere were outraged. Egyptians were livid with anger. In essence, foreigners again decided what Egyptians should have decided. This time, foreigners voted—actually stole—a portion of Egyptian land and openly gave it away.

Cadets march in formation at the Egyptian Military Academy in Cairo during the 1940s, around the time when Hosni Mubarak entered the academy and began his military career.

Of Prayers and Guns

A t 19 years of age, Mubarak left the Nile Delta and the tiny village of his youth and began his military career at Cairo's prestigious Military Academy. Meanwhile, Egypt, Lebanon, Syria, Jordan, and Iraq declared war on the newly created nation of Israel. Mubarak was too young to participate in the fighting, but the hostilities that spawned it would later shape his life.

The 1948 war was about much more than 8,000 square miles of dusty soil and rock. Anger erupted from deep within Arab and the Jewish souls. Each fought for his own country's religious, historical, and cultural heritage as much as for the 256-mile long strip of land that the United Nations chose to call Israel. As long as the blue Star of David unfurled above Palestine, the Arabs and Israelis bloodied the land that three world religions regard as holy.

RELIGIOUS ORIGINS OF CONFLICT

Ironically, Arabs and Jews share a common ancestor. The Arabs claim their lineage to Abraham through Ishmael. God had promised Abraham a son. Because Abraham's wife Sarah was past childbearing age, she gave her Egyptian handmaiden, Hagar, to Abraham. Their child, Ishmael, was Abraham's firstborn. Miraculously, Sarah herself later bore a son, Isaac. Following God's instructions, Abraham and Sarah moved to Canaan. Hagar and Ishmael remained behind in what is now Saudi Arabia. The Prophet Muhammad, originator of Islam, was born of Ishmael's line centuries later. The Jews' claim on Palestine (called Canaan in the Bible) began when Abraham left Ur in the Fertile Crescent for the land that God promised him and his descendants.

Isaac's son, Jacob (later called Israel), sired 12 sons. The 12 tribes of Israel were named after them. The words "Jew" and "Judea" originated from the name of Jacob's fourth son, Judah. Jacob's sons kidnapped Jacob's favorite son, Joseph, and sold him to the Egyptians as a slave. Joseph became an advisor to the pharaoh and saved Egypt from a great famine. When the famine spread to Canaan, Jacob, his other 11 sons, and their families moved to Goshen in Egypt. They flourished there until a new pharaoh enslaved them.

In 1280 B.C., Moses led the Hebrews (children of Israel) out of Egypt back to the land they believed Jehovah (God in the Old Testament) promised them. En route, Jehovah gave Moses the Ten Commandments on Mount Sinai. These principles, the foundation of the Jewish religion, were carried in the Ark of the Covenant (a chest or box representing God) toward the Promised Land (Canaan or Palestine). The Hebrews finally entered the Promised Land behind Joshua. The Hebrews unified under a formal government and were ruled notably by King Saul, King David, and King Solomon. In Jerusalem, Solomon built a glorious temple to house the Ark (and the tablets with the Ten Commandments).

The Jews in Palestine were conquered by the same invaders who conquered Egypt: the Assyrians, the Babylonians, Greek Alexander the Great, and the Romans. The Jews rebelled against their Roman rulers many times. And the Romans expelled the troublemakers many times, sending large groups to Alexandria. The Jews, who had turned to trading, then immigrated to other countries. This was called the *Diaspora,* Greek for "scattering," which meant the scattering of the Jews to countries outside Palestine. Though they no longer lived in Palestine, the Jews continued believing that the Promised Land, having been given to them by Jehovah, was both their spiritual and geographic homeland.

During the time of the Romans, Christianity developed. While Jews believe Jesus of Nazareth was a wise rabbi (or teacher), the Christians believed he was the Messiah, the Son of God. His teachings are in the New Testament of the Bible. Jerusalem and Palestine are also special to Christians for the many sacred sites of the 30 years when Jesus Christ lived there.

The Arabs swept across Palestine in the seventh century in a *jihad* (holy war). They took Palestine, Persia, Iraq, and eventually Egypt (in A.D. 639). Muslims, followers of Islam, also considered Palestine holy ground. Islam is based on the teachings of Muhammad the Prophet. Islam's holy book, the Koran, also contains stories about Jesus and Old Testament prophets. Controlling Palestine, the Muslims built the Dome of the Rock where Muhammad ascended to heaven. Unfortunately, the shrine covered the Moriah Rock, where the Jews believed Abraham nearly sacrificed Isaac in obedience to Jehovah, and where the Temple's sacred chamber, "The Holy of Holies," is located, which Jehovah himself visited. The Muslims also converted a Christian basilica dedicated to the Virgin Mary into the El Aqsq Mosque. The three religions were literally stacked on top of each other.

Christians and Jews were generally tolerated by their

Palestine is considered holy ground by the Muslims, Jews, and Christians alike, which has sparked holy wars and disputes for centuries. The Muslims built the Dome of the Rock mosque, pictured here, on the Moriah Rock, a sacred Jewish site.

Muslim conquerors until Turkish Seljuks came to power in the eleventh century. The Turkish Seljuks attacked Christians on pilgrimage to Jerusalem. The violence that resulted from devout men over their religion's holy places staggers, consider-ing many of the instructions in the Jewish Torah, the Muslim

Koran, and the Christian Bible. The first rule in the Jewish Ten Commandments, the Five Pillars of Islam, and the teachings of Jesus Christ calls believers to worship one God.

"HOLY" WARS AND CONFLICTS

Seven crusades followed. For nearly 200 years, earnest Christians who had learned, "Love your neighbor as yourself" slashed and whacked their swords through Muslims. Muslims, who are directed to act charitably, impaled the Christians. Jews, who are instructed, "Thou shall not kill" also fought ferociously. The crusaders and the Muslims alternately dominated the Holy Land and Jerusalem. When the Muslims finally retained control, Suleiman the Magnificent rebuilt parts of Jerusalem and allowed Jews to return and rebuild their homes. While Palestine then ricocheted from the Ottoman Turks, to Napoleon, to Egypt's Muhammad Ali, and then back to the Ottomans in 1840, Muslim Arabs claimed Palestine as their spiritual and geographic home.

Meanwhile, Jews throughout the world dreamed of returning to where their hearts had always been. Hungarian journalist Theodor Herzl moved that dream toward reality. Believing anti-Semitism (prejudice against Jews) would never go away, Herzl wrote that Jews should have their own country, and that country should be Palestine. Writing "The Jewish State" in 1896, he called Palestine a "country without a people" and the Jews "a people without a country."

Jews began immigrating to Palestine in great numbers. Britain, already occupying Egypt to safeguard the Suez Canal from the Germans in World War I, liberated Palestine from the Ottoman Empire in 1917. More Jews rushed to Palestine. Britain signed the Balfour Declaration, which suggested that Palestine become the Jewish homeland, barring harm to existing non-Jewish communities or the current residents' civil rights. That was a tricky business. How could Britain allow land that was already occupied by Arabs be given to the Jews without upsetting the Arabs?

Palestine wasn't such a great place to call home. Soil had eroded, forests had been cut down, and sand dunes piled high, blocking streams from reaching the sea. Marshes and swamps covered what could have been fertile farmland. But the Jews, invigorated by the world's increasing acceptance of Zionism, worked hard at improving the land. New immigrants from Poland and Russia poured into the country.

THE JEWS LOOK FOR A HOME COUNTRY

By 1928, the year Hosni Mubarak was born, Jews were a culture within a culture, developing journals in the Hebrew language, erecting a university, a theater, and institutes. Jews outnumbered non-Jews in Palestine 872,700 to 156,000.

Britain talked out of both sides of its mouth. Realizing Arab residents resented the influx of Jewish immigrants, Britain tried to close the country to immigration. One ship, the *Exodus*, arrived at Palestine with 4,515 immigrating Jews. From the ship's windows, they could see Palestine, but the ship wasn't allowed to dock. Instead, the *Exodus* and its refugees were sent to France. France also did not want the disappointed immigrants. The ship traveled on to West Germany, where the passengers were forced off the boat. Media coverage of the refugees' plight angered the rest of the world.

The Egyptians, always hungry to govern themselves, saw Nazi interest in their country as a way to throw off British control. In 1942, Rommel, the German commander in charge of Africa, came within 65 miles of Alexandria. Cairenes (people of Cairo) celebrated in the streets. Members of the Egyptian army, including Gamal Abdel Nasser and Anwar Sadat, tried to reach Rommel to work with him. Bungled messages thwarted the effort, and the British defeated the Germans.

At the end of the war, Britain still controlled both Egypt and Palestine. Conflict in the British Mandate of Palestine

Israeli soldiers patrol a road during the Israeli War of Independence. On the day that Israel declared its independence, the Israel army defeated the armies of Egypt and other members of the Arab League.

escalated between the Palestinian Arabs and the immigrating Jews. The population of the two groups reversed. In 1917, 50,000 Jews lived among 600,000 Arabs. By 1948, 200,000 Arabs lived among 650,000 Jews. Many Arabs left Palestinian territory and ended up in refugee camps in Lebanon, Syria, Jordan, Egypt's Gaza Strip, and the West Bank.

CONFLICTS CONTINUE BETWEEN ARABS AND JEWS

The summer before Hosni Mubarak entered the National Military Academy, the United Nations divided Palestine into two states—Jewish and Arab. As far as Arabs were concerned, Palestine was all theirs. Jews were elated. In slicing up the country, Egypt was to get the Gaza Strip. Jerusalem was to be an international city.

On May 15, 1948, the day after Israel proclaimed its independence, Egypt, Lebanon, Syria, Iraq, and Transjordan (members of the Arab League) attacked Israel from three directions. The upstart nation thoroughly defeated the Arab armies. In fact, in addition to winning the war, Israel enlarged its territory, taking lands that were originally designated to be part of the newly formed Arab state. Egypt agreed to sign an armistice in February 1949. This happened just as Hosni Mubarak completed a three-year military training program in two years, and he received his bachelor degree in Military Science at the Military Academy.

The animosities between the Arab countries and Israel continued. The humiliation the Arabs felt in defeat changed the climate in the Middle East forever. Egyptian soldiers later learned they were doomed from the beginning, sabotaged by their own government. High-ranking officials in King Farouk's government were corrupt. Money that was supposed to have purchased new weapons for the Army simply disappeared into the hands—and bank accounts—of King Farouk and his friends.

". . . we learned that the enemy was lurking not only in the night before us, but was also entrenched in our cities behind us—traitors of our own blood," said Mohammed Naguib, a twice-wounded war hero. "Weapons were delivered to our troops, but minus vital parts . . . Medical supplies for our wounded, and they were many, came through to us in pitiful quantities. Many items of field equipment desperately needed by fighting men never arrived at all."

NASSER CREATES THE FREE OFFICERS MOVEMENT

Major Gamal Abdel Nasser also fought honorably in the 1948 war. He had been wounded in the shoulder and nick-named "Tiger of Faluja." But he was more than a brave soldier;

he was a natural leader who spoke out for his beliefs. During high school, he organized a demonstration against the British. Stationed in Assiut after he graduated from the Royal Military Academy, he even campaigned against his superiors. "The senior officers were very bad," he said. "I organized all the junior officers into a group against them."

Like Naguib and many other Egyptians, Nasser was fed up with his government and the British-backed king. King Farouk flew in barbers from Europe to cut his hair. He ate 30-egg breakfasts, flirted with showgirls in Cairo's nightclubs, and gambled (against the Koran's directives) in Monte Carlo. So Egypt's political party, Wafd, fought him for control. Anti-British feelings rose again. The Muslim Brotherhood increased terrorist activities. The war did not end for the Palestinians who fled their homeland. Women dressed in black walked through groups of listless children and idle men playing pebble games in the sand.

Nasser turned his organizational skills against Farouk's government by secretly hand-picking soldiers and forming a covert organization called the Free Officers Movement.

"I was patient and never despaired," he later said. "I chose them one after another and tested them without their ever knowing it."

The Free Officers Movement eventually numbered over 700 men, who secretly gathered information to overthrow the government. Anwar Sadat was among them.

Lieutenant Hosni Mubarak was far removed from this smoldering political discontent. Too young to be noticed for the Free Officers Movement, he entered the Air Force Academy to become a fighter pilot. A former classmate remembers, "Control and precision are two of his strongest traits. He is basically a military strategist."

During the revolution against British control, Egyptians in Cairo called for a boycott of British goods during a parade in memory of Egyptians who were killed by British forces during riots.

4

A New Egypt

For Hosni Mubarak and for Egypt, 1952 was a pivotal year. In March, Mubarak graduated from the Air Force Academy as an expert in flying British Spitfires, and he was sent for additional flight and bomber training in the Soviet Union. A full-fledged fighter pilot and squadron commander, he returned to the Air Force Academy as an instructor.

Meanwhile, the political and religious unrest that smoldered throughout Egypt finally burst into flames. More interested in the orchids and apricots in his several palaces than in the welfare of Egyptians or Egypt's position in the world, King Farouk was despised by the people he was supposed to govern almost as much as they despised the British who governed him.

THE REVOLUTION

For years, Nasser—now Colonel Nasser—and the secret Free Officers Movement had gathered information from a spy network that reached into the king's palaces, army officers' conversations, and every level of the government. Although the Free Officers had planned to take over the government in 1955, events soon escalated this timetable.

In 1951, tensions increased between Egypt and Britain. Canceling the 1936 Anglo-Egyptian Treaty, Egypt's prime minister started an Egyptian boycott of the British. Workers, railroad engineers, customs officials, merchants, and businessmen quit servicing the British. The *fedayeen* (Arab commandos), with secret support of the Egyptian Army, harassed the British. In January 1952, the British retaliated by attacking rebellious police in Ismailia. Ordered to stand their ground, the police force was cut down.

The next morning, Cairo burned. With the help of the Muslim Brotherhood, a student demonstration against King Farouk turned into a full-scale riot. Department stores, restaurants, and foreign businesses were set on fire. The luxurious hotels where foreigners liked to throw lavish parties were firebombed. By the time "Black Saturday" ended, 40 people were dead and hundreds injured. Rumors spread everywhere: the army was about to revolt; the Muslim Brothers would lead a coup. Farouk, terrified of the rumors, reorganized his Cabinet officials. Nasser, seeing an opportunity, moved the Revolution up to some time between July 22 and August 15.

The Free Officers surrounded King Farouk's palace with field guns and tanks. On July 23, 1952, at 7:30 A.M., Nasser asked Anwar Sadat to inform Egypt about the Revolution over the radio. "Egypt has gone through a difficult period in its recent history, which was plagued by bribery, graft and corruption," he said. "The corrupt elements were responsible for our defeat in the Palestine War. That is why we have carried out a purge. The Army is now in the hands of men in whose ability, integrity and patriotism you can have complete confidence."

By 11:30 A.M., Nasser's bloodless revolution against the monarchy was accomplished. Sadat, the man who would eventually lead Egypt, wanted to execute the king. But Nasser's less violent opinion prevailed. Three days later, "His Majesty" signed documents announcing his abdication. Terrified for his life, Farouk misspelled his own name and had to sign twice. His life spared, he sailed into exile with his queen and his children and hundreds of suitcases. He left behind several residences—one with 400 rooms—coin collections, hundreds of suits, and gold holders for his Coca Cola bottles.

Egypt had endured 2,284 years of conquest and domination, political maneuverings, and strategies. It had been ruled by kings, caliphs, sultans, and emperors. It had seen the armies of the Hysoks, Persians, Greeks, Romans, Muslims, Fatimids, Ayyubhids, and Ottomans. It had fought British control for nearly 75 years. At last, with Gamal Abdel Nasser, Egyptians were in charge of Egypt.

With so many of his supporters below the rank of lieutenant colonel, Nasser knew the organization needed an experienced man whom the Egyptians would recognize. He chose as a figurehead leader in Major General Mohammed Naguib, the Commander in Chief of the Egyptian Armed Forces and a hero of the 1948 war. So, Naguib became president and prime minister. Nasser became deputy prime minister. Naguib declared Egypt a republic. The first army general to hold the office, President Naguib first eliminated threats to the new government. He placed a "quarantine" on all political parties for one month. He jailed leaders of the powerful Wafdist party and Muslim Brotherhood.

The bloodless overthrow of King Farouk's government left many of Farouk's supporters both in the government and in the army. Not sure whom he could trust and whom he could not, Naguib removed many from office. Although Hosni Mubarak

Egyptian President Gamal Abdel Nasser waves to the crowd on June 19, 1956, celebrating the end of martial law after the forced abdication of King Farouk.

and officers of his generation didn't yet know it, the purge of the older, more experienced officers cleared a path for a quick rise into authority and power.

Egypt's leadership changed in 1954. Nasser, the real leader of the revolution, became prime minister and in November replaced Naguib as president. Nasser's revolution was a house-cleaning revolution. He and his Free Officers wanted to get rid of British interference, the king's rule, and the power of the rich landowners. Most of Egypt's 21 million citizens loved Nasser. He talked their talk and walked their walk. The son of a postman, he spoke everyday Egyptian rather than the classical Arabic language.

CHANGES IN THE ECONOMY AND EDUCATION

Nasser wanted to improve the lives of the common people. His economic plan called for increased government spending on education, seizing all foreign-run schools, and providing government jobs to university graduates. For once, the poor felt a compassionate hand in their lives. The government subsidized their rents and food, keeping food costs low. They received free health care.

Best of all, Nasser broke up the large landholdings of the wealthy elite, limiting them to 200 acres. Before the takeover, 2% of the people owned 50% of the land. His Agrarian Reform Act made it easy for even the most humble Egyptian to own a small parcel of land. The huge tracts of land were divided into five-acre lots, enabling some of the 8 million *fellahin* to purchase land for the first time. Before the Revolution, many farmers had worked for only five Egyptian pounds a month, while landowners grew rich. As sons and relatives of the farmers themselves, army officers of the Revolutionary Command Council happily supported the plan.

Still, the quarreling factions within Egypt were a worry. Although all political parties had been banned by Naguib two years earlier, the Muslim Brotherhood continued to operate, shrilly calling for the merger of Islamic and Egyptian law. In 1954, a Cairo plumber and member of the Muslim Brotherhood fired eight shots at President Nasser. The crackdown on the organization was immediate and brutal. Leaders were tortured and executed. Four thousand Brotherhood members were sent to concentration camps.

Nasser's foreign policy was littered with diplomatic land mines. After so many centuries of foreign interference and domination, it was not surprising that Nasser wanted no intervention of any kind from foreign powers. He rejected foreigners' prying into Egyptian affairs; yet he liked the money they could give his country. He courted both Western bloc countries and Eastern bloc countries, but would not make an alliance with either. In a policy he eventually called "positive neutrality," he negotiated with both to gain the best advantage for Egypt.

THE ASWAN HIGH DAM AND THE SUEZ CANAL

One project Nasser hoped to finance was the building of the Aswan High Dam on the Nile River. This would increase water supply for irrigation and provide hydroelectric power. It would allow *fellahin* to grow three crops where they had previously grown one. It would make 2 million acres of desert into productive land. And it would provide the electronic power for a new industrialization in Egypt.

The negotiations had high stakes. At first, Great Britain and the United States agreed to supply $270 million for the first stage of the project. Nasser asked for military aid as well. They were willing to comply as long as Egypt allowed Western military advisors to, in essence, supervise Egypt.

Having just created an Egyptian-run government, Nasser had no intention of relinquishing control to foreigners again. He turned to the Soviet Union, who eagerly signed an arms agreement with him. Giving Egypt military aid gave Russia a foothold in the Middle East. Angered, the Western powers withdrew their offer to finance the Aswan Dam. Israel grew alarmed at the Soviet shipments of planes, submarines, tanks, and guns. They suspected the weapons were earmarked for Israel.

On July 6, 1956, Nasser played his trump card. He seized the Suez Canal Company from its British and French owners, claiming that the revenues from the canal would pay for the Aswan High Dam in five years. On the fourth anniversary of the revolution, Nasser announced, "In the name of the Government of Egypt, I inform you that the Suez Canal Company is nationalized and I have come to take over the premises."

Having lost their easy access to Middle East oil and the

lucrative revenues from the canal, the French and British were outraged. They froze Egyptian assets in their banks. They sent 200 warships to "convince" Egypt to return the canal. Israel joined the British and French cause. Meanwhile, things were not going well between Egypt and Israel. After groups of Palestinian raiders—some from Egypt's Gaza Strip— had crossed Israel's borders, Israel retaliated. Since 1950, Israel had been barred from using the canal (in violation of a treaty guaranteeing all countries passage through it). Israel sent paratroopers into the Sinai Peninsula. Two days later, the British and French bombed Egyptian airfields. Egypt's new Soviet-made planes were destroyed. Egypt was devastated. It lost both the Sinai Peninsula and the Suez Canal in the fighting.

The Soviets, Egypt's primary military benefactors, threatened to intervene at the Suez Canal. Nasser appealed to U.S. President Dwight D. Eisenhower, who was furious that his Allies had not informed him of their intentions. He was fearful that if the Soviets directly attacked France and Britain, the United States would have to intervene and the result would be World War III. He pressured them until they relinquished their new positions, leaving a United Nations peace-keeping force to patrol the Egtyptian-Israeli border.

The Arab world admired Egypt and Nasser for their initiative. Nasser had lost the Suez War militarily, but he did triumph over Britain, France, and Israel. They were forced by the United States, another formidable superpower, to return the Suez Canal.

Nasser's most grandiose dream was to unite the Arab world. He planned to bring all Arabs, then all Africans, and then all Muslims under his leadership. The closest he came to these goals occurred in 1958. Fearing a Communist takeover in Syria, he persuaded Syria to unite with Egypt to form the United Arab Republic. But three years later, Syria left the partnership.

French troops patrol Port Said during the Suez Canal conflict in 1956.

MUBARAK IS NOTICED

During Egypt's international maneuverings, Hosni Mubarak was diligently performing his job, teaching at the Air Force Academy. He was a strict disciplinarian who went by the book and took no nonsense from others. But while Mubarak did not seek a political career, politicians were soon noticing him. During his seven-year career as an instructor, Mubarak trained Hafez el-Assad, the future president of Syria. Another of his students was Anwar Sadat's brother, a member of the

Revolutionary Command Council. Mubarak treated him just like any other student. "I didn't want anybody to think that he had privileges," Mubarak said. "I hate people who exploit the fact that anybody in their family is important." When Sadat came to watch his brother perform, Sadat was so impressed that he wrote Mubarak's name down in a notebook for future reference.

During this time, Mubarak also met Suzanne Sabet, whose brother was also a student. Mubarak and the half-Welsh, half-Egyptian woman became engaged in 1957 and married in 1958. Being a military wife meant ". . . seeing him packing up in the middle of the night to go on a mission." She said, "You have to live with it and just try to push it away from your mind, but it is there. . . . It was a very hard life."

With the Soviets supplying arms to Egypt, Mubarak was put in charge of all Soviet-made bomber aircraft. He made several trips to the Soviet Union—in 1959, 1960, and 1961—to train in the Ilkyushin-28 and Tupolev-16 bombers.

Egypt supported the communist rebels that fought against Royalist forces, like these soldiers, during the Yemen civil war. Mubarak commanded the Egyptian Air Force during this war.

The Cost of War

I n 1962, Hosni Mubarak's military career and political future veered closer together with Egypt's involvement in Yemen's civil war. Stung by the departure of Syria from the United Arab Republic in 1961, President Nasser attempted to rebuild his tarnished image among his Arab neighbors.

MUBARAK IN THE YEMEN WAR

Anwar Sadat suggested helping Yemen. He convinced Nasser that supporting the Yemen army's coup against their monarchy would involve "just a few planes tossing bombs out of the windows." So Nasser put Sadat in charge of the Yemen campaign. It was, however, more complicated than Sadat's analysis. By supporting the communist rebels, Egypt opposed the powerful and wealthy Arab country of Saudi Arabia, which supplied money and arms to the royalists. This in turn placed Egypt in opposition to the United States, who backed the Saudis. By helping the rebels, Egypt lost the considerable aid that the United States had been giving as well as vital shipments of wheat. Moreover, Egypt underestimated the royalists' resolve to hold on to the country. What Sadat thought would be a "picnic on the Red Sea" eventually involved one-third of the Egyptian military and stretched on for five years from September 1962 to December 1967.

Hosni Mubarak, now a highly regarded instructor, was sent to command the Air Force units that fought in the Yemen War. Mubarak performed well. So much so that in 1964, Nasser appointed Mubarak head of Egyptian military delegation to the Soviet Union for advanced training at Moscow's Frunze Military Academy.

"After we were nominated, Nasser called us in," a fellow trainee recalls. "And he told us that he had only one request: he wanted us to return home as anti-Communists."

Nasser needn't have worried. Mubarak never forgot how the delegation was treated. Under heavy surveillance, its movements were restricted, and it was required to take a course in the history of the Communist Party. Worse still, it wasn't shown any of the Soviet Union's advanced technology. Later, when Mubarak commanded the Egyptian Air Force, he vowed to never use MiG-23 fighters "even if the Russians give them to us free."

The Egyptians' 14-month stay away from home also revealed Mubarak's strict moral code. Mubarak, who had been married for six years, advised the members of his delegation, "If you are married and have a girlfriend, it means that you don't respect your family."

MORE CONFLICTS IN THE MIDDLE EAST

The Middle East was the world's largest political brushfire. Just when one hot spot seemed to be put out, another would flare up. U.N. peace-keeping forces maintained an uneasy peace for a decade with the Israelis. But six months of PLO (Palestine Liberation Organization) raids into Israel (supported by Jordan and Syria) intensified the tensions. Israel retaliated swiftly, as always. In November 1966, Israel struck 30 miles inside Jordan, claiming that el-Samu was a PLO stronghold. Then on April 7, 1967, in a shoot-out above Damascus, the Israelis brought down six Syrian MiGs. Claiming Syria might need a harsher lesson, the Israeli prime minister said, "It is quite clear that Syria is the focal point of terrorists and we shall choose the time, place and means to counter the aggressor."

Because of its pact with Syria, the prime minister's words hit close to Egypt. "How can I fight Israel with 50,000 men in Yemen?" Nasser asked. But taunted by his Arab allies and assured by his defense minister that everything was ready for a confrontation, Nasser dispensed Egyptian troops on May 15 to the border where the Israeli army was amassing.

ISRAEL ATTACKS EGYPT

Three days later, Nasser called for the withdrawal of U.N. forces from Egypt. Then on May 25, Nasser closed the Gulf of Aqaba to Israeli ships and ran a media campaign, asking why the world had no sympathy for Palestinian rights. Arabs praised his stand. But his actions fanned the smoldering crisis into an inferno.

Israel had already announced that closing the Suez Canal would result in war. On June 5, 1967, the Israelis struck. Their attack hit all air bases from Alexandria to Egypt's capitol at the same time. Israeli jets flew over Cairo skies during morning rush hour. Houses shuddered and glass rattled in the windows. Roads filled with cars, buses, and bicycles as people hurried to get to their homes or into air-raid shelters. Air-raid sirens screeched. The ground thudded. Black smoke rose in the distance.

At first, the Egyptian public thought they would win the war. Cairo radio stations announced the number of downed

Israeli planes. People danced in the streets. Then, the devastation sunk in as world media told the truth, and the wounded returned with their horrifying stories.

Although the fighting continued for six more days, for all practical purposes, the war was over in 80 minutes. Egypt's air force and defense systems were completely annihilated where they sat on the ground; 309 of 340 aircraft were destroyed.

With no air cover, the Egyptian army fought a lost cause. "Our soldiers were cut down where they stood," one soldier recalled. "We didn't even get a chance to fire a shot," said another. The army retreated across the Suez Canal, followed by the finely honed Israeli military. Israeli jets flew over Cairo for four days, sometimes bombing, sometimes setting off sonic booms that rattled apartments and shattered glass. Their troops at the Suez Canal were a mere 60 miles from the capital.

Mubarak had been at Cairo West Airfield as commander of the capital's main air base since 1964. In the initial attack, he quickly ordered his pilots south, to the cities of Luxor and Aswan. As a result, his squadron was one of the few still operational.

By the time the June 11 U.N. cease-fire went into effect, 10,000 Egyptians had died. Israel captured the Gaza Strip and Sinai Peninsula from Egypt; the West Bank of the River Jordan from Jordan, and Syria's Golan Heights, tripling the size of Israeli territory and adding a million Palestinians to their jurisdiction. Jerusalem, regarded by Muslims as nearly as sacred as Medina and Mecca, was completely controlled by the Israelis. (Cities located in Saudi Arabia, Mecca is the birthplace and Medina the burial place of Mohammed, the spiritual leader of Islam.)

DEFEAT OF EGYPT AND THE EGYPTIAN SPIRIT

Just as the Japanese attack on Pearl Harbor affected every American, the Israeli assault irreparably seared the Egyptian psyche. Nearly every Egyptian family knew the dead or the wounded. The Egyptian military was branded by shame. Egypt

Israeli tanks and bombers in southern Israel forced the Egyptian army to retreat across the Suez Canal in 1967. Israel's victory tripled its territory.

had been surprised, and, more grievously, unprepared. But unlike Pearl Harbor's infamy, Egypt had no means to avenge the Six-Day War. Egypt lost, and the memory of the defeat would remain an open, weeping, infected wound for another half decade.

Two days before the cease-fire, Nasser addressed his nation on the radio, admitting Egypt's defeat and announcing his resignation. People ran into Cairo's streets by the tens of thousands. For 17 hours, they demonstrated, encircling

Nasser's home and chanting, "Nasser. Nasser. We are with you. We will not accept defeat." The National Assembly persuaded him to stay in office. The defense minister was removed and later committed suicide. Gamal Abdel Nasser did govern three more years, but he was a broken man, both in body and in spirit. In essence, the Nasser era ended with the Six-Day War.

In the aftermath, the Soviet Union replaced some destroyed equipment and installed surface-to-air missiles along the Suez Canal. These defensive weapons, however, did not help to rebuild the air force. Neither did the 20,000 Russian technical advisors, who filled Egyptian cities once again with foreigners.

Nasser was beleaguered with problems from all sides. By losing the Sinai Peninsula, Egypt lost its oil wells and their income. The Suez Canal, a major source of Egypt's revenue, was blocked by sunken ships. And tourism to Egypt's historical treasures understandably dropped off. Egypt's defeat undermined Nasser's leadership with the other Arab nations who could help Egypt financially.

EGYPT'S EFFORTS TO CLEAN UP AND REBUILD

As the shock of their loss wore off, Egyptians realized the defeat had been a glaring contradiction of all the Nasser government had promised—military supremacy, political change, and social reform. The Muslim Brotherhood redoubled its attempts to become a bona fide opposition party. Nasser moved to cleanse the government of corruption and power hoarders and to punish the military leaders for their incompetence. Purging the military became another opportunity for Hosni Mubarak to be noticed by Egypt's political leadership. Remembering his quick thinking in saving Egyptian planes, Nasser elevated him to Director of the Air Force Academy in November 1967.

In June 1969, Nasser appointed Mubarak as Air Force

Chief of Staff. His most daunting assignment was to rebuild the decimated air force. The same month, Nasser's health crumbled, and he suffered his first heart attack. Six months later, Nasser appointed the sometimes inept, but always loyal, Anwar Sadat as his vice president. It was to be a temporary, largely ceremonial appointment while Nasser was out of the country attending the Arab summit conference in Rabat. Nasser believed the Socialist Union and the army would really manage the affairs of state. "Besides," he told journalist Mohamed Heikal, "all the others have been Vice-President at one time or another; it's Anwar's turn."

Nasser had other pressing issues on his mind. By hoping to reconnect with the West, and, in particular, the United States' financial aid, Nasser was forced into another fray with the Arabs. Weary of their hard-line no-war-no-peace policy, Nasser wanted a political settlement with Israel. In June 1970, he announced that Egypt was ready to seriously negotiate under Secretary of State William Rogers' plan. But the Palestine Liberation Organization (PLO), based in Jordan, embarked on a series of violent raids and hijackings directed at Israel. Jordan's King Hussein, thinking the PLO posed a threat to his own government, attacked and drove the PLO out of his country. Instead of fighting their common enemy, Israel, the Arab leaders fought each other.

In September 1970, Nasser convened an emergency meeting with Arab leaders in Cairo. The four-day conference went so badly that Nasser collapsed just after it ended. Suffering his second heart attack, Nasser died at home on September 28. Vice President Sadat made the sad announcement on television. "I bring you the saddest news of the bravest of men, the noblest of men," he said. "President Gamal Abdel Nasser has died after a brief illness which modern medicine has failed to cure."

The entire Arab world mourned his passing. Egyptians were hysterical. Five million people lined the funeral route. The

The coffin holding the body of Egyptian President Gamal Abdel Nasser moved slowly through crowds of mourners on October 1, 1970, in Cairo, Egypt.

crowds were so thick, it took an hour to move Nasser's coffin 100 yards.

Why Egyptians so venerated Gamal Abdel Nasser was, in a way, a contradiction in common sense. During his tenure in power, Egypt lost two wars at great cost to the country's economy and dignity. The Suez Canal was closed, costing Egypt $600 million in revenue. Egypt under Nasser was never a democracy or a republic, and Nasser was a dictator of enormous power. Mail could be opened; political enemies could be banished to desert concentration camps; candidates for office were hand-picked by Egypt's hero. And 23,000 political prisoners, many of the Muslim Brotherhood, languished in jail. The *fellahin's* lifestyle changed little even though more of them owned land. The birth rate was unmanageable.

In other ways, the great affection of the Egyptian people was very understandable. Nasser ended the foreign domination of his country. He ruled for 18 years. He outmaneuvered both his Egyptian and world enemies. Some of Nasser's plans paid off. Industry's contribution to the national output increased from 10 percent to 21 percent during his administration. He reclaimed the Suez Canal for Egypt and built the Aswan High Dam, which opened in 1968. The ratio of doctors to people improved from 1 in 5,000 to 1 in 2,000. Life expectancy increased from 43 to 52 years of age. Ironically, Gamal Abdel Nasser was exactly 52 when he died.

SADAT BECOMES PRESIDENT OF EGYPT

Egypt's third president, Anwar Sadat, was virtually unknown to the Egyptian public. Government officials who watched him busy himself around Nasser as a public relations man and Nasser's aide ridiculed him. The only person who took him seriously was Anwar Sadat himself.

"You have invested me with an honour which, God knows has never crossed my mind throughout my life; nor have I striven for it," he assured Egypt's Parliament after he became president. "My programme is Nasser's." In another 11 years, Egypt would hear this disclaimer and this pledge again—not about Nasser but about Sadat, not spoken by Sadat but by Hosni Mubarak. Through Anwar Sadat, the forces of destiny would intervene in the quiet life of a quiet military career man, and he didn't know it yet.

Anwar Sadat was president of Egypt from 1970 until his assassination in 1981.

6

The Problems of Peace

nwar Sadat had been vice president just nine months when President Nasser died in 1970. Few politicians actually respected Egypt's number two man. If anything, they thought he would be a weak president and could be easily manipulated. What Egyptians did know was that life was very hard for most of them and that all Egyptians wanted the land Israel had taken from them in 1967. Early on, Sadat was told that Egypt's highest priority was "the struggle to liberate Arab land . . . everything should be sacrificed for the sake of victory."

Sadat spent 1971 shoring up his position as president. He appointed Ali Sabri as his vice president. Sabri was supposed to develop the power base for Sadat's regime. Instead, the pro-Soviet radical and his cohorts mounted a conspiracy to overthrow Sadat. When the president outwitted the coup, his control of Egypt was legitimized. Sadat then replaced officials with those who would be loyal to him.

At the same time, Sadat was dealing with the Israel problem. He called for a three-month extension of the U.N. cease-fire, yet spoke militantly about the need for progress in Israeli-Egyptian negotiation. Rejecting the cease-fire, he added that "it wasn't necessary that diplomatic activity will stop and that the guns alone will speak."

The fact was, however, that Egypt had no guns. The Six-Day War had destroyed Egypt's weaponry. The Soviet Union, which Sadat never really liked, was still Egypt's main source of military aid. But Russia was trying to establish a peaceful relationship with the United States and was slow to deliver equipment. This frustrated Sadat. He repeatedly traveled to Moscow during 1971 and 1972, trying to speed up the process. In the spring of 1972, Leonid Brezhnev (general secretary of the Soviet Communist party) had promised an arms shipment, which had yet to arrive by July. Then, Russia sent Sadat a message saying "there was no point arming Egypt because Egypt was not capable of winning a war against Israel in any case."

A furious Sadat expelled 15,000 Russian military advisors and technicians. Egyptians were glad to be rid of a foreign presence in their country. Their president had finally stood up to the superpowers. Sadat's popularity soared.

Sadat's global decision was yet another small step in Hosni Mubarak's future. For when an Egyptian general complained about the Russian expulsion, Sadat gave the general's job, Deputy Minister of War, to Mubarak. Already Air Force Chief of Staff, Mubarak was also promoted to Commander in Chief of the Air Force. Mubarak's first duty in his new position was to accompany Sadat to Russia to seek more aid.

Sadat was after something more important than weapons or Egyptian bravado. Sadat was shrewdly remaking Egyptian policy. He wanted to regain the Sinai Peninsula and other land

Israel had wrested from the Arabs. To accomplish this, Egypt needed a closer relationship, both diplomatically and financially, with the United States and with Europe.

At first, Sadat seemed willing to negotiate a peace treaty with the Israelis. He proposed a return to the pre-1967 borders and a plan addressing the Palestine refugees. In return, he offered to recognize Israel's right to exist. He called 1971 "The Year of Decision," when Egypt would get its demands through peace or war. He blustered through 1972, talking about going to war with Israel, but war never came. By 1973, Israel and its allies disregarded Sadat's words. True, their intelligence reports indicated a military build-up by the Arab world. But they thought Egypt would never attack the unbeatable Israeli army. Sadat, who had talked for so long without doing anything, had become the boy who cried wolf.

SURPRISE ATTACK ON ISRAELIS

The Egyptian people badly misjudged their president. Sadat had really been laying an elaborate smokescreen to confuse the Americans and the Israelis. For all his radio and television appearances, for all the newspaper articles that detailed what the army had yet to do before going to war, Sadat had really been planning a surprise attack on Israel. The army trained for Operation Badr all through 1973. The soldiers didn't know it, but their practice—23 rehearsals in all—was secret training for the coming war. In fact, they had practiced so often that the Israelis, who could see their tactics from their side of the bank, quit paying attention.

As commander in chief of the Air Force, General Mubarak was to plan the air attack that would start the war. Mubarak's planes were to provide air cover for an assault on Israeli positions on the East Bank of the Suez Canal and the Sinai Peninsula. Mubarak's assignment in Sadat's surprise war was formidable. Most of the Egyptian air planes—300 of its 340— had been destroyed in the 1967 war. The MiGs that the

Russians sold to Egypt to replace them were not state of the art like the planes the French and Americans supplied the Israelis. But Mubarak had been an excellent instructor, and he had trained many of the Egyptian pilots. "He knew all his pilots and officers, their fitness, their personal life and professionalism," an aide later recalled.

Mubarak's plan was brilliant. On the pretext of maneuvers, he called in every available plane. He outfitted the unarmed training planes with cannons and rockets. On the fateful morning of October 6, 1973, Egyptian troops stationed across the Suez Canal lounged along the West Bank. They pretended to relax, fishing, swimming, and sunbathing. A skeleton crew of Israeli soldiers manned positions across the water. It was shaping up to be a quiet day in both Israel and Egypt.

In Jerusalem, city life stood still. Businesses were closed; the radio stations were silent; synagogues were full of worshippers observing Yom Kippur, the Jewish Day of Atonement. In Cairo, Muslims waited for the signal when they could eat. They were commemorating Ramadan, when Muhammad the Prophet received the words of God for the Koran. Fasting from sunrise to sundown was part of the month-long celebration.

A propaganda lie that was broadcast over the radio informed Egyptians and Syrians that Israeli warplanes and gunboats were attacking in retaliation for Palestinian guerrilla raids and hostage taking. After military and patriotic songs, more radio propaganda reported "our air force carried out its duty with success and scored hits on enemy positions." *That* announcement was true.

Streaking low, Egyptian planes flew over the Suez Canal, headed toward Israeli headquarters, communications, and electronic targets. They dropped bombs and rockets and sprayed buildings with machine guns. The 100° heat shimmered with explosions. Egyptian sunbathers were replaced by 2,000 Egyptian guns. Surface-to-surface missiles

Hosni Mubarak planned the air attack that began Egypt's surprise attack on the Israelis during the Yom Kippur War in 1973. Egypt won a psychological victory, enabling it to negotiate with Israel from of position of strength.

launched and fell at supersonic speeds on the Israeli positions. The planes flew on to the Sinai Peninsula. They particularly wanted "Budapest," a lookout east of Port Fuad where Israel could monitor Egyptian naval movements.

Mubarak's plan was precisely and meticulously executed. The planes hit 90 percent of their targets within 20 minutes. As the planes returned from their missions, 8,000 Egyptians pushed off in hundreds of rubber rafts and crossed the canal. They scaled the Bar Lev Line. The 40-foot tall, 110-mile long dirt wall was so formidable that experts thought only an atomic bomb could destroy it. Egyptian soldiers let down rope and bamboo ladders for other soldiers and positioned howitzers, anti-tank, and anti-aircraft missiles. The Israelis—all 436 men left defending the fortifications—were dumbfounded. One hysterical radioman yelled, "Hundreds, thousands of Egyptians are swimming toward our fort. We need reinforcements, quickly."

The lightning strike was not without casualties. The Egyptians lost some planes and pilots, including Sadat's brother. But the Egyptian pilots performed superbly, protecting the infantry as it crossed the Suez Canal and attacking the 50 strong points and rear posts along the Bar Lev Line.

To get Egyptian tanks across the canal and beyond the Bar Lev Line, the Egyptian Engineers Corps used powerful fire hoses. Spewing 1,000 gallons of water a minute, they gouged out sixty 20-foot-wide holes in the earthen wall for pontoon bridges. Within 24 hours, five divisions of Egyptians were entrenched on the East Bank of the Suez Canal. In all, 120,000 men, 2,000 tanks, and 700 aircraft participated in the attack. U.N. observers reported that Egyptians crossed into the Sinai Desert from five points along the 103-mile canal.

Mubarak's contribution to the surprise attack was unquestioned. Without a successful air strike, 26,000 Egyptians would have died. Instead, only 180 died in the first assault. Sadat later said, "Hosni Mubarak worked wonders . . . . The Egyptian Air Force achieved an epic feat—heroic and glorious."

The war was actually a cooperative Arab effort. Syria 250 miles north committed 100,000 men. Between 1,300 and 1,400 Syrian tanks advanced through the Israeli-held Golan Heights. The Shah of Iran sent a half-million tons of oil. For once, 17 Arab nations were united, not squabbling among themselves.

EGYPT GAINS RESPECT

The Egyptians were ecstatic. They gathered in the streets, on rooftops and on balconies to celebrate. Egyptian planes had shot down world opinion from the sky. They obliterated the idea that Egyptians were cowards and grossly inept. They wiped out the idea that Arabs could not cooperate. The surprise attack returned to Egypt—and their Arab neighbors—the pride and honor they had lost from the 1967 staggering loss to Israel. The people reacted: Men formed long lines, trying to enlist; women offered to help the Red Cross; volunteers gave blood.

Outside Egypt, Sadat and Egypt immediately acquired a new respect from both the Soviet Union and the United States. For the first time, Egypt could negotiate with Israel from a position of strength. The Soviets were more than happy to quickly supply Egypt with more weaponry. The United States immediately felt the tightening of King Faisal's hand on Saudi Arabia's oil spigot when he ordered a 10 percent cutback and then a complete stoppage of oil shipments to the United States.

CEASE-FIRE

Egypt and Syria, while winning an important psychological victory, could not win the war. The United States rallied to its ally, Israel, by sending over $2 billion in new weapons, tanks, and bombs. Resupplied, the extraordinary Israeli military machine put the Egyptians on the defensive. Within four days, Israel had regained the Golan Heights from Syria and had come within 20 miles of the Syrian capital and 45 miles from Cairo. The United Nations announced a cease-fire on October 16. Although at a military disadvantage by this time, Sadat was still willing to fight Israel but not to take on the United States.

Sadat sent Mubarak to his Arab allies to explain Egypt's reasons to stop fighting and negotiate with Israel peacefully.

"Mubarak didn't change anybody's mind," an Egyptian official said later, ". . . but they got to know and respect him."

A broken cease-fire continued until December 22 when U.S. Secretary of State Henry Kissinger issued an ultimatum: If Egypt attacked the Israeli-occupied West Bank, the United States would directly intervene. Egypt put down its guns.

The war had its cost. In 19 days, Egypt lost 15,000 soldiers; Syria lost 3,500 men; Israel lost 2,700 men and 150 planes.

Representatives from Egypt and Israel gathered near Cairo for peace talks, which resulted in the end of the Yom Kippur War.

Peace, like love, may be in the eye of the beholder. All parties involved in the war had different visions of what a peace treaty must include. Israel wanted to be recognized by its Arab neighbors. Egypt wanted to regain the Gaza Strip and Sinai Peninsula that were lost in 1948. All Arabs wanted Jerusalem to be an international city. The Palestinian Arabs wanted a homeland.

For their part in the war effort, Mubarak and other military men became known as the October Generation. Mubarak was called a hero and would later be promoted in February 1974 to Air Marshal of the Egyptian Air Force.

MUBARAK ENTERS POLITICS

The next year, Mubarak ended his military career for a political one. Sadat fired Vice President Hussein Shafei. He had been Sadat's political adversary and one of the last members of

Nasser's Revolutionary Command Council. Remembering the assassination of King Faisal, Saudi Arabia's leader, Sadat realized he needed a vice president to head the government if he met the same fate. He appointed Hosni Mubarak, a man who symbolized a new kind of Egyptian—self-confident and certain he was the Israelis' equal.

Announcing Mubarak's April appointment, Sadat said, "We want a new generation to step forward to the country's leadership. We want this generation to express the spirit of October 6th."

Hosni Mubarak (in khaki uniform) stands next to President Anwar Sadat (in white). Mubarak had never held a political position before Sadat named him as his vice president; the appointment surprised many Egyptian politicians.

7

The Invisible Man

I need a Vice President who will share with me state responsibilities at all levels. No one can foresee the future, and state secrets must not be known by one person alone.

ANWAR SADAT, PRESIDENT OF EGYPT

Anwar Sadat had surprised everyone by appointing Hosni Mubarak as his vice president. Like Sadat, Mubarak was dismissed by politicians as just another aide who would parrot, "Yes, Mr. President." Who could blame them? Mubarak had held no other political position. He was a political unknown. Yet, if they had looked closely they could have taken the measure of his character.

Mubarak was a military man through and through. He was punctual and thoroughly prepared. He wasn't afraid of hard work or discipline. He completed his assignments and managed minute details well. He and his wife Suzanne lived modestly with their two sons in a Cairo suburb. Instead of indulging in the customary Cairo afternoon nap, he preferred playing squash. Just as the October War proved, he was smart. He realized he had much to learn as vice president. He quietly settled into the chairs behind Sadat and listened carefully, laughing politely at Sadat's jokes and taking meticulous notes. He was so unobtrusive that U.S. Secretary of State Henry Kissinger mistook Egypt's second in command for a junior aide.

"At times he seemed more like Sadat's messenger boy than heir apparent," said one Western diplomat.

But Mubarak was definitely more than that. Sadat hated to do tedious paperwork and to read reports. Mubarak soon handled the details of day-to-day government. He presided at Cabinet meetings and headed Egypt's intelligence services and rearmament program. By appearing at ceremonial functions and ribbon cuttings, he freed Sadat to work on the complex problems of Egyptian economy, Israel, and the Arab world. Still, critics called him "Sadat's Sadat," the "court jester," and even *La Vache Qui Rit* (The Laughing Cow) after a bland French cheese spread.

Within one year, Mubarak was much more than a paper pusher. As the president's representative, he intervened to end the guerrilla war in the Western Sahara between Morocco and rebels seeking independence. He headed an official Egyptian delegation to the People's Republic of China seeking spare parts for Egypt's MiG fighters. As vice president, he was the highest-ranking Egyptian to visit China. He was sent to get a troop withdrawal from Syria and Iraq after fighting broke out along the Syrian-Iraq border.

EGYPT'S DIPPING ECONOMY

Egypt's government faced monumental problems. In rural areas, farmers still used short-handled hoes and blind-folded buffalo from the time of the pharaohs. Forty percent of the

The disparity in the standard of living between Egypt's rich and poor reached its zenith during the 1980s. Cairo's population soared, and many found themselves living in abject poverty.

men and 60 percent of the women were illiterate. Modern Cairo, built for 3 million, was bursting with 5 million people. Migrants from the country arrived in Cairo's population at a rate of 1 every 90 seconds. In the available housing, there were 3.7 people in every room. A half-million people lived among the gravestones and mausoleums in the "City of the Dead." Great wealth and appalling poverty existed side by side. City streets were used by herds of goats and sheep as well as 250,000 cars. Markets stocked caviar but not flour or soap. Hostesses in Edwardian mansions served afternoon tea and candlelight dinners, while children in the slums drank from sewers and were preyed upon by rats. Some Cairenes lounged about at poetry readings; others worked for $30 a month.

In fact, Egypt was going broke. Sadat, who believed prosperity followed peace, later admitted that the 1973 war, in part, had been a way of distracting the people from their hardships. But the war itself had cost Sadat financial resources. When he expelled Soviet advisors, Russia cut off direct aid to Egypt. When he agreed to a Egypt-Israeli cease-fire, he lost Egypt's Arab allies and their finances. Egypt had yet to forge a strong relationship with the United States, the world's richest country.

RIOTS IN THE CITIES

Once a great wheat exporter, Egypt couldn't feed its own people and was forced to import wheat and rice. It was difficult to feed so many mouths and dangerous not to. Hungry mouths could turn into a mob. One such mob demonstrated in front of the luxury hotels, yelling "Oh Hero of the Crossing, where is our breakfast?"

Striking textile workers who ate primarily bread and beans, broke into their supervisors' homes to find large quantities of whiskey and frozen turkeys. Sadat responded by lowering food prices, arresting corrupt officials, and increasing luxury taxes.

In January 17, 1977, the government announced cuts on basic necessities such as bread, rice, and beans to reduce the billion dollar cost of food subsidies. Demonstrations turned to protests; protests turned to riots. Hundreds of thousands of people filled the streets. Those living in back-alley shanties as well as middle-class bureaucrats, students, and workers burned government buildings and looted boutiques and nightclubs. They destroyed buses, ripped up railroad tracks, and smashed imported luxury cars. The crowd and those watching from the rooftops chanted, "Sadat, O Sadat, you dress in the latest fashion, while we sleep twelve to a room."

Sadat was at his winter resort in Aswan, preparing for a

visit from Yugoslavia's president when the rioting broke out. He didn't know until the next day about the riots in Alexandria, Cairo, and all the other major cities. With rioters headed to get him, Sadat quickly returned to Cairo. Egypt was so close to civil war and Sadat so close to losing his presidency that the presidential plane and a helicopter were readied for his escape to Iran.

Although Sadat had promised never to ask the army to turn on Egyptians, he asked the army to bring the rioting under control. The army agreed reluctantly, on the condition that the subsidy cuts would be reversed. By the time the army restored order, 160 people had died, 1,000 were wounded, and 5,000 were arrested. But Sadat's presidency had been saved.

Some Arab nations as well as the United States sent emergency money to help Egypt. But Egypt's economy could not be fixed so easily. The discontent and desperation of the people merely melted into the shadows, back to militant groups like the Muslim Brotherhood and the Gama, who hoped to overthrow their president.

Most disturbing of all were the Muslim mullahs (teachers of sacred law), dressed in white prayer robes and waving the Koran, who had been among the rioters. Political and economic unrest had turned religious. Many Islam leaders wanted reform—a return to fundamentals spelled out in the Koran.

SADAT SEEKS PEACE WITH ISRAELIS

Nine months after the riots, another event catapulted Egypt into the international spotlight. On November 9, 1977, Sadat made an astonishing offer in a speech to the Egyptian Parliament.

"... I am prepared to go to the end of the world—and Israel will be surprised to hear me tell you that I am ready to go to their home, to the Knesset . . . in order to prevent one Egyptian soldier from being wounded . . . "

The world was shocked. Sadat was offering to break the Egyptian law that forbade Egyptians to deal with Israelis in any way. He was offering to go to a place that was described only on Egyptian maps as Occupied Palestinian Land. He was offering to make peace with the enemy, those illegitimate trespassers of Arab land who had once humiliated the entire Arab world.

Arab countries were livid. Even Syria, Egypt's largest military ally in the October War condemned the offer. Yasir Arafat, the leader of the Palestine Liberation Organization (PLO), left Egypt and never returned.

Six days after Sadat's announcement, Prime Minister Menachem Begin invited Sadat to Israel. Sadat crossed the uncrossable chasm between Egyptian and Israeli, between Muslim and Jew in a 28-minute flight from Egypt to Tel Aviv. En route he told a *Time* journalist, "What I want from this visit, is that the wall created between us and Israel, the psychological wall, be knocked down."

When Sadat arrived at the airport on November 19, 1977, Egypt's flag and Israel's flag flew side by side. He was greeted by Prime Minister Begin, former Prime Minister Golda Meir, General Moshe Dayan, who had masterminded the 1967 war, and Ariel Sharon, the general who broke through Egyptian lines in 1973. Huge crowds lined the road, waving posters and shouting Sadat's name.

The next day Sadat prayed at the el-Aqsa Mosque, Islam's third most holy shrine, visited the Christian Church of the Ascension, and later addressed the Knesset (Israel's parliament). In his speech, he outlined the requirements for peace: a withdrawal from the lands Israel took in 1967 and a recognition of the Palestinians. In return, he said, " . . . I declare it to the whole world, that we accept living with you in permanent peace based on justice." It was the most important thing for Israel: recognition as a country.

Whether Sadat's motive was peace for the Middle East, increased United States involvement in the region, or American dollars for the Egyptians, the Israelis could no longer argue that Sadat was out to murder every Jew. They had to meet him at the peace table.

THE COST OF PEACE

Sadat received a hero's welcome from his people, but the Arab leaders were not so thrilled. Libya's Muammar el Qaddafi (also Gadhafi) broke diplomatic relations with Egypt. In Tripoli, Libya citizens burned Egyptian offices to the ground. Palestinians near Damascus, Syria, burned Sadat's pictures and threw bombs at the Egyptian Embassy. In Spain, Palestinians seized the embassy and held the Egyptian ambassador hostage. They seemed to forget that Egypt always paid the highest price in men, machinery, and emotions. With poverty and overpopulation squeezing Egyptians from all sides, the 28 percent of the national budget spent on wars was needed in other places.

Working out the details of peace was grueling. Overcoming decades of suspicion and hatred was exhausting to both Israel and Egypt. Despite the many meetings held between the two governments, real progress was both very slow and anguishing. Neither wanted to concede, but both demanded much.

After conferring separately with Sadat and Begin, U.S. President Jimmy Carter invited both leaders meet at Camp David in September 1978. For nearly two weeks, they haggled over terms. On September 17, they finally announced some broad agreements. Egypt agreed to establish diplomatic relations with Israel. Israel agreed to withdraw from Egypt's Sinai peninsula and set up means for resolving the future of the Gaza Strip, the West Bank, and the Palestinian issue. A month later, October 27, 1978, Menachem Begin and Anwar Sadat, who was already honored as *Time*'s Man

Egyptian President Anwar Sadat, U.S. President Jimmy Carter, and Israeli Prime Minister Menachem Begin shake hands on the north lawn of the White House in Washington, D.C., after Egypt and Israel signed a peace treaty on March 26, 1979.

of the Year, were jointly awarded the Nobel Prize for peace.

Bringing both countries to the table to actually sign the treaty had yet to be accomplished. One issue was the return of the Sinai's rich oil fields to Egypt, but Israelis feared they would run out of fuel. Only when Egypt agreed to be a major supplier and America guaranteed Israel's oil supply for 15 years was the treaty actually signed. On March 26, 1979, Sadat, Begin, and Carter met again to make the peace official.

The peace cost Egypt alliances with other Arab nations. They called Sadat a devil and peace with Israel a heresy. When Sadat refused their collective bribe of $5 billion, Saudi Arabia and Syria allowed personal attacks in the press and Libya's Qaddafi threatened to kill Sadat.

When U.S. President Jimmy Carter lost his reelection, Sadat could no longer count on aid from the United States. As Sadat's troubleshooter, Vice President Mubarak made two trips to the United States in 1980. He said goodbye to Jimmy Carter and met with the new president, Ronald Reagan. Mubarak urged speeding arms to Egypt's neighbor, Sudan, which Cairo believed was threatened by the radical regime of Muammar Qaddafi in Libya. Within Egypt, Mubarak was elected to vice chairman of the National Democratic Party, the organization that selected Egypt's presidents. This broadened Mubarak's political power. Significantly, while other politicians and government officials were appointed and later relieved of their positions, Mubarak survived.

Aware that assassination plans always swirled through Egypt, Vice President Mubarak tried to dissuade Sadat from appearing at the celebration that commemorated the victory of the 1973 October War. But Sadat flatly rejected the idea. He also refused to wear his bulletproof vest, claiming it ruined the lines of his new London-made uniform. Believing himself safe near the army, he expected the October 6 military extravaganza to be a wonderful day. Unfortunately, he was wrong.

Hosni Mubarak became Egypt's fourth president on October 6, 1981 after the assassination of Anwar Sadat. Mubarak's first task as president was to stop the militants who were rioting in Egypt.

8

Wait and See

"I am not an ambitious man at all," Mubarak said, echoing Sadat's acceptance speech 11 years earlier. "I didn't ask to be President. I just accepted it because it is in the interest of the country. . . . I look to the post for its responsibilities, how to tackle the problems and solve them. This is my only interest."

Eight days after Sadat's assassination on October 6, 1981, 53-year-old, Hosni Mubarak became the fourth president of Egypt. It was a job he hadn't really wanted.

The challenges began even before he was nominated by the Egyptian parliament and elected by the vote of 12.5 million people. For three days, October 8 to 10, the militants rioted with security forces in Assiut, Upper Egypt.

PAYING TRIBUTE

Leaders from all over the world flew to Cairo for the funeral of the slain Sadat. The United States sent three former presidents—Gerald Ford, Richard Nixon, and Jimmy Carter. Even Prime Minister Menachem Begin flew from Israel, grieving not only for Sadat the president, but Sadat the friend and partner in peace. President Mubarak and Sadat's son Gamal led the funeral procession to the Tomb of the Unknown Soldier where Sadat was buried.

While the world honored their president, Egyptians themselves were very subdued—at least compared with the hysteria they displayed at Gamal Abdel Nasser's passing. Some flags flew at half-mast in Cairo's streets. Pictures of the president were plentiful, but not draped in the black mourning cloth that should have hung over them. Some people offered prayers for his soul, but the mosques were not overly filled.

"The feeling right now is that despite the violent way it came about, there's actually a sort of relief that Sadat is gone, said one expert. "His popularity was at an all-time low. The economy seems to be caving in. It's an attitude that seems alien to the Egyptian character, but there it is."

THE NEW PRESIDENT

Mubarak, the tactician and problem solver, acted quickly. To prevent more violence during Sadat's funeral ceremonies, he imposed a 40-day ban on mass meetings and marches. No more than five people could gather together at one time. He also directed a one-year state of emergency. He announced a firm determination to stop militants and any other disturbances to the public; 350 suspected members of Islamic militant organizations were arrested. Eventually 3,000 would be detained. After inter-rogating Sadat's assassins, the government learned militants had infiltrated Egypt's most powerful group—

the Egyptian army. Forty officers and 100 more enlisted men were discharged.

The United States didn't know what to expect from a Mubarak presidency. Mubarak had met and negotiated with The United States in the past. He had made frequent trips, requesting that the United States speed up arms deliveries of the $3.5 billion order that Egypt had placed. Just five days before Sadat's assassination, Mubarak had been in Washington, D.C., asking for military aid for Sudan, Egypt's southernmost neighbor, which was being threatened by Libya. He told American officials that the Soviet-armed Libya and "Soviet aggression" in Chad, Ethiopia, and South Yemen were the most dangerous threats to Egypt.

Three decades before, Gamal Abdel Nasser had aligned Egypt with the Soviet Union. After relying on Russia for military aid and becoming disillusioned about their help, Sadat developed a strong relationship with the United States. He had even offered to allow American rapid-deployment forces to use Egyptian military facilities if the Soviets moved to control the region or its important oil supplies. This was critical to the United States.

"If we couldn't get to the Gulf through Egypt, with overflights for example, we'd be in very serious trouble," said U.S. Secretary of State Alexander Haig.

Egypt's Arab neighbors knew Mubarak primarily as the vice president who once said "everything should be done quietly and not in a dramatic way." With 400,000 in the armed forces and 43 million people, Egypt should have been the Arab world's leader, in what Mubarak called "a vanguard role." But the other Arab nations hated Sadat. They felt that Sadat had betrayed them by communicating with Israel. Worse, he had insulted them, once calling critics of his peace initiative "dwarfs." So the other Arab nations had broken diplomatic relations with Egypt and

Many Arab nations disapproved of Sadat's communication with Israel, and Egypt was expelled from the Arab League and the Islamic Conference Organization, pictured here. However, with Mubarak as president, many Arab nations considered readmitting Egypt to these organizations.

expelled Egypt from their own organizations, the Arab League and the Islamic Conference Organization. Even so, individual Arab countries disagreed with each other about readmitting Egypt with Mubarak leading the country. Some analysts believed Saudi Arabia and Jordan might reestablish contact with Egypt's new low-key president. For Mubarak, a friendship with Saudi Arabia could result in access to the Saudis' vast oil fortune. However, Libya, Syria, and the Palestine Liberation Organization (PLO) were hard-liners. Conveniently forgetting they had thrown Egypt out of their organizations in the first place, they wanted Mubarak to approach them, asking to mend their broken relationships. They also wanted Mubarak to reject the Camp David Accord. They wanted Egypt to fight—with weapons or with words—for the rights of the Palestinians. They never stopped believing that Israel was their worst enemy. They waited to see what Mubarak would do after the last section of the Sinai, lost to Egypt for 15 years, was returned in April.

"We made a peace treaty with Israel and we will not go backward," President Mubarak said bluntly. "We are not prepared to lose our children in war at a time when we are advancing toward peace. The wars are over. That is it, enough."

Israel, had already returned two-thirds of the Sinai Peninsula before Sadat's death, and the deadline for returning the final third was in six months. But other issues between the two countries were far from resolved. Many Israelis fiercely opposed giving the Palestinians the West Bank or the Gaza Strip. Some thought Mubarak could be pressured by the Arab countries to make different concessions. After the April transfer, they didn't know what would happen between Egypt and Israel.

STATE OF THE ECOMONY

Egypt was left in an appalling condition because of Sadat's preoccupation with regaining respect for Egypt's military and establishing peace with Israel. The country had a civil debt of $19.5 billion and a military debt of $5.7 billion—a total of over $25 billion, which was ten times greater than at the beginning of Sadat's presidency. Of Egypt's 43 million people, nearly 41 million lived in awful poverty. Cairo was still bursting with people. One riot between Muslims and Coptic Christians began because one family's laundry had been dirtied by another family's waste water. And still, Egypt's population increased by 1 million each year. The average Egyptian earned a paltry $630 a year (about $1.83 a day) compared with the average American's $12,000 a year. College graduates were hired by the government and paid $17 a month (about $.07 an hour in an eight-hour day). Public services were in a shambles. Unable to feed its own people, Egypt imported three-fourths of the nation's wheat.

"It's all a matter of just wait and see," said one Cairo businessman. "That's what most Egyptians are prepared to do just now—wait and see."

WEEDING OUT MILITANT GROUPS

Held in check by Mubarak's firm measures, fundamentalist and militant groups seethed, waiting to strike out at the government at any opportunity. These Muslim fanatics believed the corruption within the government and huge extremes between wealth and poverty among the people could be solved only by returning to a strict, religiously dominated government. Their infiltration into the ranks of the army was a dangerous sign. Militant groups at universities had caused several riots on campuses. And the half-century-old Muslim Brotherhood had increased its membership to 4,000 in Egypt with additional sympathizers elsewhere. Their spiritual leader had been executed in 1965 after an assassination attempt on then President Nasser. The organization continued a *jihad* (holy war) against the government. "They are a Moral Majority with AK-47s," said a U.S. official.

Mubarak warned the militants in his inaugural speech, "Anyone who thinks he can mess about with the rights of the people . . . not one of them will escape ruthless measures."

Every problem inside and outside Egypt was of near-emergency proportions, and each needed Mubarak's attention first.

"All I dream of now is of continuing President Sadat's Administration," he said to a journalist. "We can turn the country green, we can find the homes for our people, we can finish the peace process and see our land returned to us. But truthfully, I haven't yet the time to think over such things."

Obviously, Mubarak's top concern was Sadat's assassins. At first, Mubarak thought the four men who stepped outside that truck and murdered his president were acting alone. But many unexplained questions implied a terrorist plot. How did live ammunition get into the parade? How did the truck conveniently end up at the end of the convoy and on the side nearest the reviewing stand? Why did the attack begin just as everyone focused on the planes? Investigations followed. Two thousand militants were arrested and questioned. A special military court convened in November for those accused of murdering Anwar Sadat and seven others. Twenty-four men were tried, including the man who had cried "I am Khaled Islambouli. I have killed Pharaoh, and I do not fear death." Found guilty, Lieutenant Islambouli and four other assassins were sentenced to death.

On the other hand, Mubarak showed balance and fairness when he released some of the 1,500 protesters and suspected troublemakers whom President Sadat had jailed in his crackdown three months earlier. Among them was the noted journalist Mohamed Heikal, a feminist leader, several Muslim Brothers, teachers, lawyers, and writers who did not deserve to be arrested or brought to trial.

"He [Sadat] arrested many people, fundamentalists and politicians, but his assassination changed the situation," Mubarak said in an interview. "I have to start another way of

Suspects in the assassination of Egyptian President Sadat were apprehended on October 6, 1981, and sentenced to death.

dealing with the people. I have to release those who are not dangerous. I have to release the politicians. I have to confer with the other parties here so that all of us can work for the benefit of the country."

Becoming president under such circumstances was like

walking on gelatin. With each step, Mubarak didn't really know what kind of support he could expect. Even military support was doubtful. The generals were unaccustomed to being led by an air force man. To ensure a loyal army, Mubarak transferred, retired, and dismissed officers he suspected did not support him.

MUBARAK SETS DOWN A NEW WORK ETHIC

Mubarak's first major speech to Parliament signaled where his attention would lie. "Our aim, should be to serve the interest of the masses. Our ultimate aim should be to set up a society of purity and justice, and not a society of privileges and class differences and exploitation," he said.

The stern, no-nonsense president set the tone for his new administration. Sadat had worked about four hours a day in the garden outside his home. He began at 11:30 A.M. and ended with an afternoon walk, a massage, and a nap. Mubarak's workday varied from eight to sixteen hours. He instructed the Egyptian Parliament to work harder and made them clock in and clock out. He told them they would forfeit pay for unexplained absences and could not leave during a debate. He ordered his government ministers not to accept personal gifts from other officials and forbade them to themselves give gifts valued over $120.

Sadat had depended on a large circle of advisors, two of whom were his sons-in-law, and others who had become wealthy during his administration. Mubarak told these men their services were no longer needed and brought in experts from outside the government.

Sadat had been flamboyant and charismatic. He ruled by personality as much as by power, promoting a father-figure image to his people and a visionary man of peace to the world. He loved parties and all the luxuries of the presidency. Mubarak, on the other hand, had lived quietly and modestly as vice president. He displayed awards and mementos of his

Mubarak's first speech to Parliament set the tone for his administration: he had a strong work ethic, and wanted the members of Parliament to adopt the same attitude.

military career. An introvert, he was uncomfortable with small talk receptions and the glare of spotlights on his life. Upon becoming president, he told journalists, "I don't want you to call me an Air Force hero or my wife the First Lady. There is no First Lady—there is Mrs. Mubarak, and my children are not the President's children. They are two boys—themselves."

The "First Family" remained so obscure that Mrs. Mubarak

completed her dual masters degree in sociology and anthropology without either professors or fellow students knowing she was the President's wife. Mrs. Sadat, on the other hand, took her comprehensive exams for her degree on Egyptian television.

Hosni Mubarak was Egypt's new president. He brought a new style and new demeanor to Egypt's ageless problems. The whole world waited to see how much or how long he would succeed.

Mubarak grappled with the same problems Sadat faced during his presidency, including the tension between Israelis and Arabs, the revitalization Egypt's economy, and whether or not Egypt should accept aid from the U.S. and risk alienating fundamentalists.

9

The Frying Pan and the Fire

"When every chicken lays an egg, must I be present for the photographer," President Hosni Mubarak impatiently asked an aide. Egypt's fourth president possessed none of his predecessor's showmanship. He didn't enjoy the presidency's pomp and pageantry. Besides, there wasn't any time for picture taking.

Mubarak was in the hot spot no matter where he turned or what he tried to do. He faced the same difficulties both Sadat and Nasser had faced. If Mubarak advanced the cause of peace with Israel, he would further alienate the Arab world. If he sweet-talked the Arab countries, he would upset Israel. If he accepted aid from America, the radical fundamentalists protested. If he allowed the fundamentalists to make Islamic law the basis of government, the Christian Coptics would rise up. If he raised food prices to save the government, then the people would riot. If he kept prices low so the poor could buy food, he could bankrupt Egypt.

WHAT MUBARAK DID *NOT* DO

Mubarak's approach was vastly different from Sadat's. What Mubarak did *not* do in his first full year in office was as significant as what he *did* do. He did *not* plan lavish military extravaganzas (like the parade where Sadat was murdered). He did *not* wage war on any Arab state. He did *not* verbally insult Arab leaders. While sect rivalries and protests continued, he did *not* provoke civil war. President Mubarak did *not* perform in front of the media. He gave only four speeches from October to February. They were direct and succinct.

"His ideas are crystal clear, his speeches very short," said a former Sadat confidant. "This gives a picture of his mentality—brief, mathematical and logical."

Mubarak did *not* tolerate the widespread corruption in Sadat's government. Because Sadat's *infitah* or open-door policy encouraged foreign investors, many Egyptians, including Sadat's own half-brother, had become rich. The bus driver turned multimillionaire was convicted, along with several other Sadat family members and friends, fined, and jailed. Mubarak warned his own relatives not to buy influence with the Mubarak name. He replaced Sadat's old cronies with new faces. He appointed two Christian Coptics.

Outside Egypt, Mubarak did *not* allow the peace process to unravel.

"I studied all the details of the peace process," he said. "I knew everything that was discussed, even the most confidential meetings between Mr. Begin and President Sadat. I supervised the whole peace process and if anything went wrong I tried to correct it."

CONTINUING RELATIONS WITH ISRAEL

A month before Israel returned the Sinai's final section, Mubarak reassured the Arabs that Egypt's relationship with Israel did not threaten their objectives. At the same time, he reassured Israel. There was about as much chance of Mubarak being manipulated as the Sphinx moving. He said, ". . . I never accept pressure from any foreign power at all."

On April 25, 1982, Israel returned the last section of the Sinai. Although he did not appear at the ceremony, Mubarak justifiably called it a "magnificent achievement." Mortal enemies had faced each other, worked out an agreement, and honored their word.

Those who thought Egypt would distance itself from Israel after the Sinai exchange were disappointed.

"We are not going to change anything . . . We have sacrificed a lot for peace," Mubarak said shortly before the April 25 hand-over. "We don't intend to overthrow it. We are looking forward to much better relations with Israel."

Likewise, those who thought Egypt would distance itself from everyone else to be allied with Israel were also wrong.

"You are a very strange people," Mubarak told an Israeli journalist. "You want us to have peace with you and to have no relations with anybody else? We are part of the Arab world, and for hundreds and hundreds of years we've had good relations with it."

Still, important issues needed to be resolved. The Palestinians' right to a homeland and self-rule had the highest priorities for Arabs—demands Israel refused to give. Ownership of Taba was another unresolved problem. Its 700 yards of beach had been disputed since a British surveyor drew the Palestine and Egypt's boundary with a fat lead pencil. Eighty years later, Egyptians claimed Taba, having lost it in the 1967 war. Israel claimed it because an Israeli luxury resort was erected there.

MUBARAK'S POLICY OF NONALIGNMENT

Mubarak did *not* completely make Egypt an ally of either America or Russia. While Nasser had been pro-Soviet and Sadat had been pro-American, Mubarak announced a new policy of nonalignment. Egypt would work with all and be obligated to no one. He asked Russian technicians to help in his new industrial projects, thus courting diplomatic relations with the U.S.S.R. Egypt supported Palestinian self-determination. But when Israel invaded Lebanon, attempting to destroy the PLO, Mubarak refused to abandon the Egypt-Israeli relationship. When the Israelis murdered hundreds of Palestinian Arabs living in refugee camps, he recalled the Egyptian ambassador from Israel. In December, Mubarak agreed to help Iraq fight Iran by selling $1 billion of arms and by perhaps sending the Egyptian army, the largest in the Arab world. Arab nations approved.

Mubarak's accomplishments during his first year as president drew mixed reviews. Once relieved that Mubarak had none of Sadat's extravagant visions, critics began calling for quick solutions to Egypt's complex difficulties. Mubarak was frustrated, especially with Egypt's economy.

"People are saying, 'The rais [boss] has been there for a year, what has he brought us?' said Mubarak. "By the Prophet Muhammad, if they brought in a government of angels, it wouldn't make any difference."

In 1983, Mubarak's nonalignment policy continued. In February, he allowed Americans to deploy AWAC reconnaissance aircraft to monitor the Libya-Sudan crisis. He also restored diplomatic relations with the Soviet Union. In December, PLO leader Yasir Arafat returned to Cairo. He had not been in Egypt since Sadat's "I will go to Israel" speech. The warming relations with Arafat had adverse affects on Israel, who called the meeting "a severe blow to the peace process. . . ."

By the end of 1983, Mubarak was succeeding in reducing tensions between Egypt and the Arab states. In January 1984, Saudi Prince Talal bin Abdel Aziz visited Egypt for the first time since 1977, and Saudi money began flowing into Egypt again. Egypt was invited to rejoin the Islamic Conference Organization. Claiming Egypt had been cleansed of Sadat's influence, Jordan reinstated diplomatic relations in September.

"All over the Arab world now people say, 'Egypt, Egypt'" Mubarak said. "Egypt is the leader, the biggest nation of the Arab world, the nation that can influence the situation more than any other. Everywhere, every day you hear the voices. 'Egypt should return.'"

Yasir Arafat met Mubarak in Cairo in 1983, and Egypt was invited to rejoin the Islamic Conference Organization in 1984. Egypt's relationship with other Arab nations was slowly being repaired after Sadat's presidency because of Mubarak's shrewd diplomacy.

MUBARAK ALLOWS OPPOSITION PARTIES IN ELECTIONS

Mubarak called the elections in May 1984 a turning point in Egyptian democracy. With his permission, opposition parties participated in the election. Nasser, fearing they were part of King Farouk's infrastructure, had outlawed them. Sadat had first encouraged them, but then he, too, feared and banned them. The only political organization was the National Democratic Party, which Mubarak as vice president headed. However, in the 1984 election, President Mubarak gave opposition parties 40 minutes on state-controlled radio and television to explain their ideas and hold election rallies. Four opposition parties appeared on the ballot—a victory in itself. Both the Muslim Brotherhood and the Wafd Party won seats. For the first time in 35 years, there were opposition voices in the Assembly—another victory.

THE *ACHILLE LAURO*, AN INTERNATIONAL INCIDENT

Mubarak regarded his integrity as his strongest asset. Known to inspect his aides' luggage for luxuries unavailable in Egypt, he found himself caught in an international crossfire. On October 7, Palestinians hijacked the *Achille Lauro*, an Italian cruise ship. Four–hundred and thirty-eight people on board were taken hostage. One disabled American Jew was killed, his body and his wheelchair thrown overboard. The Palestinians claimed the hijacking was in response to an Israeli raid over Tunis, Tunisia, which killed 65 people.

Again, Mubarak could fry in the frying pan or in the fire. If he gave the hijackers to the Americans, he squashed further friendships with Arab nations. If he didn't punish the hijackers, the United States would be outraged, and vast amounts of American aid would be jeopardized. Finally, Mubarak allowed the ship to dock in Egypt, agreeing to free the hijackers but secretly intent on sending the hijackers back to the PLO.

Mubarak explained: "In one of his statements, Arafat said 'If we receive them, we are going to put these people on trial' . . . it seemed convenient to send those people to the PLO as a test for Arafat. We had no right to put them on trial here."

But U.S. intelligence bugged Mubarak's phones and his defense minister, Abu Ghazala, revealed the escape plane's identification numbers. Four U.S. Navy F-14s intercepted the plane, forcing it to land in Sicily. The hijackers were arrested and charged with murder. Mubarak was furious. The incident was "an act of piracy" and a "stab in the back" by the United States. He called Secretary of State George Schultz "crazy." He demanded an apology for the Egyptian people. However,

Egyptian President Hosni Mubarak met with U.S. President Ronald Reagan in February 1982. The Palestinian hijacking of an Italian cruise ship forced Mubarak to walk a fine line between maintaining a diplomatic relationship with the Arabs and preserving valuable ties with the United States.

Mubarak could only "nip" at the hand that fed Egypt. The United States annually supplied $4.1 billion in economic and military aid, an amount second only to aid it supplied Israel. One of three loaves of bread contained American wheat. The American Embassy in Egypt was the United States' largest embassy. And 10,000 Americans lived in Egypt. Hundreds of M-60 tanks and F-14 fighters refurbished Egypt's military.

Relations between the United Sates and Egypt chilled until President Reagan, taking Mubarak's cue, sent the Egyptian president a letter, and a senior state department official visited him. Mollified, Mubarak sought closer military and economic aid from the Americans and participated in Operation Bright Star, a joint military field-training exercise, with them.

RELIGIOUS RIOTS

By 1986, Mubarak was again dealing with fanatic and religious forces within Egypt. In January 1985, Mubarak had intervened between the Coptic Christian minority and the Muslims. Sadat had placed the head of the Coptic Church under house arrest in 1981 after a previous eruption. Mubarak confined the pope for three years, angering the Coptic community. The conflicts continued into the summer when the two groups warred with bumper stickers. Muslims pasted "There is No God but Allah, and Muhammad Is His Prophet" on their vehicles. Coptics stuck "The Lord is My Shepherd" on theirs cars. Tensions escalated until the government fined and confiscated driver's licenses. The simmering Islamic militants bubbled over, demonstrating in the streets. Believing the government was corrupted, they called for Shari law. Mubarak arrested them. On February 25, Islamic fundamentalists erupted again. The riot began with the Central Security Forces, responding to a rumor that its recruits would serve four years instead of three, receiving $4 a month.

Normally safeguarding foreign embassies, banks, roads, and bridges, 17,000 of 300,000 members took to the streets, burning, and looting. They were joined by Islamic fundamentalists in Cairo who released prisoners from jail and burned nightclubs serving alcohol. History repeated itself when Mubarak, like Sadat, asked the army to reestablish civilian order. It took three days of intense fighting on the ground and in the air to subdue what Mubarak called "a deviationist minority." Sixty died, 300 were wounded, 3,500 people were arrested, and five hotels and 2,000 cars were damaged. All opposition parties backed Mubarak's measures and in Mubarak's freer society, the press covered the event fully.

PROGRESS AMID POVERTY

Little by little, Egypt progressed. Sewer drainage, water, and public health were improved. Mubarak's first five years produced 250 renovated factories, tripled production in electricity, 76 bridges, 3,614 miles of paved highway, and 700 miles of railway line. Telephone lines increased from 600,000 to 1.4 million. The task, however, was daunting.

The population increased without restraint. A million babies were born every eight to nine months. The foreign debt neared $46 billion. Wage increases disappeared into price increases for basic necessities like sugar, cheese, electricity, petrol, cooking gas, and clothing.

As one economist put it, "If you put all the data into a computer, it would come up with a finding that two days ago, the Egyptian economy ceased to exist."

The year 1986 did not go well. The opposition claimed that Mubarak's government was incompetent. The only opposition party supporting the Camp David Accord withdrew its recognition and joined the Muslim Brothers. A cotton pest threatened the cotton crop. The People's Assembly extended the state of emergency until 1991 because of increasing incidents with Islamic fundamentalists and militant extremists. Insurgents seemed around every corner, splintered off into increasingly radical groups. Egypt deported Iranian agents stirring up students and Palestinians agitating against the Israeli Consulate in Alexandria. The International Monetary Fund (IMF) and the World Bank criticized Egypt's dependence on foreign aid and recommended that Mubarak raise food prices. Remembering Sadat's 1977 food riots, Mubarak refused to do it.

To help, the United States released $150 million of an aid package it had delayed, hoping for more internal economic reform. America also offered to pay Egypt's $4.5 billion military debt and then refinance the remainder at lower interest rates.

EGYPT IS READMITTED INTO THE ARAB LEAGUE

In October 1987, Mubarak was elected to his second term as president. The United States sold Egypt F-16 aircraft and Sidewinders, and air-to-air missiles and resumed military exercises with Egypt's military. The International Monetary Fund approved a $300 million loan in balance of payments support. The Soviet Union resumed its economic and military aid, agreed to postpone a $3 billion debt payment for 25 years, and reopened the Soviet consulate in Port Said. In September, the French built an underground metro in Cairo.

At its meeting in November 1987, the Arab League voted to allow diplomatic ties with Egypt. Within weeks, 10 countries—United Arab Emirates, Iraq, Kuwait, North Yemen, Bahrain, Qatar, the Arab Republic of Yemen, Saudi Arabia, Morocco, and Mauritania—reestablished diplomatic relations with Egypt. Three months later, in January 1988, Tunisia and South Yemen did likewise. Only Algeria, Lebanon, Syria, and Libya refused. Prone to outrageous speech and actions, Libyan President Muammar Qaddafi once had proposed a union of Libya and Egypt, with himself in charge of the huge Egyptian army. Libya and Egypt had fought vicious border disputes. When Mubarak warned Libya that Egypt would protect the Sudan, Qaddafi retreated from Egypt's southern border. In his latest mischief, he positioned mines in the Red Sea near the Suez Canal's shipping lanes. Rumors surfaced that he planned to bomb the Aswan High Dam. Only when Mubarak warned that Libya was "playing with fire" did Qaddafi back off.

Although it was increasingly clear that peace with Israel was the government's peace, not the people's peace, Mubarak kept the Camp David Accord to the letter. He convinced Yasir Arafat to publicly renounce terrorism and recognize Israel's right to exist. Later, he tried to convince the PLO and Israel to talk directly. Mubarak even offered to visit Israel. But the meeting never came off.

In 1989, after 15 years, OPEC (Organization of Arab Petroleum Exporting Countries) readmitted Egypt. In December, Syria reconciled with Egypt. The Arab League voted to readmit Egypt, and the headquarters was moved back to Cairo. These actions signaled Mubarak's new visibility and stature in the Middle East. He had reentered the Arab fold while maintaining Egypt's formal commitment to the peace treaty.

After over a decade as president and a fourth reelection, President Mubarak still wrestles with many of the same problems that faced Egypt during his first term as president: overpopulation, militant extremists, and a struggling economy.

10

The Sameness of Sand

S o much in Egypt never changes. The sun travels a cloudless sky to set in the horizon—again. The Pyramids and the Sphinx sit through another century, waiting to be admired and studied—again. Winds blow over the landscape, rearranging a trillion grains of sand until they settle into the desert—again.

Egypt's problems never seem to change either. In 1990, after a decade under Hosni Mubarak, Egypt was still suffocating under its 55 million people. Twenty-three percent of Egypt lived in abject poverty—again. Their laundry hung from clotheslines and chicken coops cluttered the passageways—again. The national debt climbed to $46 billion. Still critical of Egypt's dependence on foreign aid, the International Monetary Fund (IMF) urged increased prices. Mubarak resisted the recommendation saying, "The IMF plan aims at killing the Egyptian citizen and is impossible to implement." Later, he tried raising bread prices in government bakeries. The people rioted—again. Three people were killed.

RELIGIOUS FANATICISM

Helplessness feeds the people's discontent, and discontent nourishes fanaticism. "The only way to stop the spread of fundamentalism," says one authority in 1981, ". . . is to end the conditions that cause it. This means tackling Egypt's desperate economic and social conditions. The trouble is Mubarak doesn't have the resources to do it." Ten years later, he still didn't. The insurgents enveloped themselves in the gallibiya's flowing robes and hijab head coverings. They believed that the laws of the Koran would free the government of corruption and foreign influence—again.

Others did not share such extremism. "How dare they?" asks filmmaker Youssef Chahine. "I do not think anyone has the right to monopolize God or his message, whether it be in the Bible, the Torah, or the Koran."

Of Islam's two groups, 80 percent of Egypt is Shiite, including the president. "I am a religious man, but not an extremist," Mubarak says. "I am a very moderate religious man."

Steadfastly refusing to legitimize extremist activities with religion, Mubarak treated militant Islamic groups as criminals in "law and order issues." In 1992, after assaults on Coptic Christians, intellectuals, security force, and police, Mubarak's response to the militants was brutal. The long-running emergency decree permitted arrest and detention of suspects without charges. Professors, lawyers, and economists were imprisoned without a trial or tried before military courts with no appeal. Five

A Muslim woman tries to make contact with a relative incarcerated by Mubarak as a Muslim militant.

thousand were arrested. Human rights activists accused Mubarak's government of allowing Egyptian authorities to torture detainees and destroy mosques and homes.

"I can assure you," Mubarak said, "these groups will never take over this country. . . . " The militants implemented other tactics, infiltrating the courts, universities, news media, trade unions, and the educational system. Seeking to replace a national identity with an Islamic one, some educators no longer encouraged singing the national anthem or saluting the flag.

"It's an immense problem," said a cabinet member. "The leaders of this movement are very well educated, and they know exactly what they want. They want to seize power, and our educational system offers them a very convenient route."

Outside Egypt's borders, Mubarak's stature increased both in the eyes of his Arab allies and with the United States. In the crises between Iraq and Kuwait, Mubarak traveled to Syria, Saudi Arabia, and Iraq, trying to resolve the crisis diplomatically. He sent medical and food supplies to the Iraqi people—which Saddam Hussein refused. After Iraq invaded Kuwait, Mubarak dispensed 43,000 troops, including 5,000 paratroopers, to the Allied Forces. Only the United States, Britain, and Saudi Arabia sent more men. Yet he declared that Egyptians would liberate Kuwait but would not enter Iraqi territory to fight.

In 1993, Mubarak was reelected for a third term. The governments of Farouk, Nasser, and Sadat all had been accused of corruption. Again, critics scrutinized Mubarak's government. They pointed to the number of Islamists that Mubarak has jailed. Human rights advocates concluded that the elections were "fraudulent," "undemocratic" and "grossly unfair." They described a group called "The Gang of Sons," who assisted Libya in circumventing U.N. sanctions. They accused Egyptian security officials of helping to return a defecting U.N. ambassador to Libya where he was executed without charges or trial.

MILITANT ATTACKS OUTSIDE EGYPT

Militant activity moved outside Egypt's borders. On June 26, 1995, Hosni Mubarak barely escaped an assassination plot in Addis Ababa, Ethiopia, where he was to attend the Organization of African Unity Conference. Would-be assassins blocked his car in the street and fired AK-47 machine guns at the armored limousine. Mubarak's driver spun the Mercedes around and security guards returned fire, saving Mubarak's life. The would-be assassins had trained in Luxor, Upper Egypt, and in Afghanistan. Once based in Iran, they obtained Yemeni passports and stayed at a Syrian "safe farm" before entering Ethiopia. The mastermind behind the assassination attempt turned out to be an Egyptian agricultural engineer and a member of the Gam'a. Mubarak returned to Cairo, outraged at the Sudanese who had supposedly shipped the attack weapons on Sudan Airways. He called Sudan's leaders "thugs, criminals, and crackpots." Egyptian and Sudanese troops skirmished for a week.

An attack on November 17, 1997, targeted Japanese honeymooners in the Valley of the Kings, British, Swiss, and German tourists who departing their tour bus for a look at the 3,400-year-old Temple of Hatshepsut. Six men in red headbands, members of the Gama'a al-Islamiya, walked in behind them. For 45 minutes, they hunted the tourists down, slit their throats, mutilated their faces, and then shot their 62 victims with AK-47 weapons. A pamphlet stuffed inside a corpse read, "No to tourists in Egypt." It was signed "Omar Abdel-Rahman's Squadron of Havoc and Destruction—the Gama'a al-Islamiya, the Islamic Group."

After commandeering the tour bus, the terrorists fought the police in a gun battle. One terrorist was wounded and then killed by his friends, who fled into the hills. None of the terrorists lived to stand trial. They died in a cave, either in a shootout with the local villagers or at their own hand. Critics believe the police shot them.

The attack was a financial blow to Egypt's fragile economy. Egypt lost at least $1.5 of the $4 billion tourist budget. Personnel affected included 700,000 tourist industry employees and up to 7 million tourist-related businesses such as souvenir stands, shops, and restaurants.

Some theorized that the militants were after more than money. The massacre's purpose may have been to so outrage the armed forces that they would step in and take down Mubarak's government. Mubarak blocked any move against his position. To reassure tourists, the government then hired a large security force to protect major hotels and tourist attractions.

FUTURE OF MUBARAK'S PRESIDENCY

Analysts believe that as long as the army supports Mubarak, his government will continue. In 1999, Hosni Mubarak was reelected as president for a fourth term. Some believe he is president for life. That he has never named a vice president reinforces this notion. Controlling the population remains a pressing domestic issue. Egypt in the new millennium bulges with a population of 63 million. Just as in the time of Nasser and Sadat, people struggle to make a living. Students finishing medical school expect to work two jobs. Because they will earn about $40.00 a month as physicians, their second job enables them to survive. Housing shortages determine when or whether a couple will be able to marry.

The Palestinian issue, after almost 60 years of conflict, still runs red with blood. After meeting with President Clinton in Cairo's airport, Mubarak said, "We are trying to do our best to find a resolution to the problem in the Middle East between Israel and the Palestinians . . . ."

Israeli Prime Minister Yitzhak Rabin (left) and Palestinian Liberation Organization (PLO) Chairman Yasir Arafat (center) shake hands at the PLO-Israeli peace accord on May 1994, while Egyptian President Mubarak looks on.

Yet two years into the new millennium, militants still blow up themselves and Israelis in Jerusalem. Terrorists have expanded the battleground into the lives of every world citizen, whether they live in Tel Aviv or New York City.

Critics of Hosni Mubarak, like the critics of his predecessors, think he is out of touch with his people, that he is surrounded by "yes" men and sycophants, and that he enjoys the luxuries of the presidency too much. His admirers, on the other hand, point to the respect others give him as Arab leader and moderator in the Middle East. In 1992, Mubarak proposed a compromise between Israelis and Palestinians. He continues his role as emissary, carrying proposals between Syrian, Lebanese, Jordanian, Palestinian, American, and Israeli negotiators. He hosts meetings between Israeli and Palestinian leaders in the peace talks. In 1996, he hosted an anti-terrorism meeting at Sharm al-Shaykh and the Arab summit.

MUBARAK THE MAN

Hosni Mubarak is an Egyptian first, an Arab second, and a Muslim third. As Egypt's president, he would not deal with Saddam Hussein's government during the Gulf War, but as an Arab he opposed dividing Iraq at the war's end. In 1995, as Egyptian president and Arab leader, he would not sign the Nuclear Non-Proliferation Treaty (NNPT) unless Israel signed also. He maintained the same position concerning chemical weapons.

Hosni Mubarak's personality has not changed in two decades. He is still tough as nails and still intensely private. While reams are written about other world leaders, Mubarak's official biography is only a few paragraphs plus a list of his honors and medals. While other world leaders live behind glass, Mubarak still lives behind a wall of smoke. Little more is known about his personal life than when he took office.

Mubarak's Egypt operates in ways neither Nasser nor Sadat allowed. Egypt's political system favors the National Democratic Party and gives powers to the president. Still under Mubarak's leadership, the opposition, even independent candidates, is allowed. Violence erupts from militants and fundamentalists. Yet Egypt has had no civil war since 1911. While Israel would wish for an enthusiastic participation in the ongoing peace talks, Egypt and Israel are not at war. His leadership in the Arab world is without question.

Hosni Mubarak's legacy has been built one detail at a time, like the granite stones of the Pyramids.

1928	Mubarak is born on May 4 in the village of Kafr-El Meselha in the Nile River Delta
1947	Mubarak enters Egyptian Military Academy in November; United Nations divides Palestine into Arab and Israeli states
1948	Israel declares independence, Palestine War (Israeli War of Independence)
1949	Mubarak graduates from the National Military Academy, enters the Air Force Academy; Israel and Egypt sign peace agreement
1952–1959	Mubarak is flight instructor at the National Military Academy
1952	Gamal Abdel Nasser and Free Officers Organization seize government from King Farouk
1953	Free Officers declare Egypt a republic
1956	Nasser nationalizes the Suez Canal; Israeli, British, and French move against Egypt
1958	Mubarak marries Suzanne Sabet
1959	Mubarak trains as a fighter-bomber pilot in the Soviet Union and again in 1961
1962	Mubarak commands the Egyptian Air Force in the Yemeni Civil War
1964	Mubarak studies at Moscow's Frunze General Staff Academy
1967	Mubarak becomes commander of the Air Force Academy and Deputy Minister of War
1969	Mubarak is promoted to Air Force Chief of Staff
1972	Mubarak is named commander in chief of the Air Force
1973	October War or Arab-Israeli war; Mubarak's execution of air strikes devastates Israel; Egyptians cross the Suez Canal
1975	April 15, Sadat names Mubarak as vice president of Egypt
1977	Sadat goes to Israel
1978	Camp David Accord where Sadat, President Jimmy Carter, and Menachem Begin discuss peace; Egypt is voted out of the Arab League
1980	Mubarak is elected to the vice chairmanship of the National Democratic Party
1981	October 6, President Anwar el Sadat is assassinated; October 14, Mubarak is sworn in as Egypt's fourth president

1982   April, Israel returns last portion of the Sinai; June, Israel invades Lebanon; September, Mubarak recalls Egypt's ambassador to Israel

1986   Central Security Forces riot, Mubarak asks army to restore order

1987   Mubarak is elected to second six-year term as president; 10 Arab states restore diplomatic relations with Egypt

1989   Egypt is readmitted to the Arab League

1991   Mubarak sends troops to Allies in the Gulf War

1993   Mubarak is reelected to third term

1995   Assassination attempt is made on Mubarak in June

1999   Mubarak is reelected to fourth term as president

Aker, Frank. *October 1973 The Arab-Israeli War.* Archon Books, 1985.

Aufderheide, Patricia. *Anwar Sadat, 1918.* New York: Chelsea House Publishers, 1985.

Cross, Wilbur. *Egypt.* Chicago: Childrens Press, 1982.

Heikal, Mohamed. *Autumn of Fury: The Assassination of Sadat.* New York: Random House, 1983.

Jones, Helen Hinckley. *Israel.* Chicago: Childrens Press, 1986.

Mirepoix, Camille. *Egypt in Pictures.* New York: Sterling Publishing Company, 1973.

Sadat, Anwar el. *In Search of Identity.* New York: Harper & Row, 1977.

Sadat, Jehan. *A Woman of Egypt.* New York: Simon & Schuster, 1977.

Solecki, John. *World Leaders Past and Present: Hosni Mubarak.* New York: Chelsea House Publishers, 1991.

Vatikiotis, P.J. *The History of Modern Egypt From Muhammad Ali to Mubarak.* Baltimore: The Johns Hopkins University Press, 1991.

Weaver, Mary Anne. *A Portrait of Egypt: A Journey Through the World of Militant Islam.* New York: Farrar, Straus & Giroux, 2000.

page:

VICKI COX is a freelance writer for national magazines and newspapers in sixteen states. In addition to two other Chelsea House biographies, she has authored an anthology of features, *Rising Stars and Ozark Constellations*, which profiles fifty people and places on the Ozark Plateau. She has an M.S. in Education, taught public school for twenty-five years, and currently teaches at Drury University in Springfield, Missouri.

ARTHUR M. SCHLESINGER, jr. is the leading American historian of our time. He won the Pulitzer Prize for his book *The Age of Jackson* (1945) and again for a chronicle of the Kennedy Administration, *A Thousand Days* (1965), which also won the National Book Award. Professor Schlesinger is the Albert Schweitzer Professor of the Humanities at the City University of New York and has been involved in several other Chelsea House projects, including the series REVOLUTIONARY WAR LEADERS, COLONIAL LEADERS, and YOUR GOVERNMENT.